YORK NOTES

General Editors: Professor A.N. Jeffares (*University of Stirling*) & Professor Suheil Bushrui (*American University of Beirut*)

EVERYMAN

Notes by Neil King

BA (DURHAM) PGCE (CAMBRIDGE)
Senior English Master,
Hymers College, Hull

D1324981

LONGMAN
YORK PRESS

For Gamps

YORK PRESS
Immeuble Esseily, Place Riad Solh, Beirut.

LONGMAN GROUP LIMITED
Longman House,
Burnt Mill,
Harlow,
Essex

© Librairie du Liban 1985

First published 1985
ISBN 0 582 79291 6
Printed in Hong Kong by
Sing Cheong Printing Press Ltd

Contents

Part 1

Introduction

The author of *Everyman*

There is no evidence in historical records, neither is there any clue in the text or in the style of the language, as to the identity of the author of *Everyman*. There is general critical agreement that either *Everyman* itself or the Dutch *Elckerlijc* (?1495)—of which it is perhaps a translation—is an original play, not derived from a French or Latin forerunner. From the evidence of such matters as rhyme-words, diction and metre it is almost certain that the Dutch play is the original of which *Everyman* is a translation. This is supported by our knowledge that in around 1500 Antwerp was a centre of printing, and that Dutch printers were busy turning out translations of Dutch books for the English market. *Everyman* may have been translated from the text of an Antwerp printer called Vorsterman. It has been suggested that the translator was one Laurence Andrewe, who came from Calais and was a bookseller in London by 1527. The only reason for this connection is that Andrewe is known to have translated books from Dutch into English, and his responsibility for *Everyman* is a mere guess.

In order to understand the place of *Everyman* in pre-Shakespearean English drama, it is necessary to survey fairly fully the development which took place from early Church playlets, through Mystery and Morality plays and Tudor Interludes.

Medieval Mystery plays

Background

Between the Roman plays of Plautus (?254–184BC) and Terence (?185–159BC) and the first plays of medieval Europe there stretches a gap of some one thousand years. During the final centuries of the Roman Empire no great plays were written, and those already in existence were read rather than acted. It seems, at first sight, that there was a complete break between the classical tradition and the rise of medieval Church drama and Mystery plays.

However, there never is a complete break in the continuity of any story. The spirit of drama was kept alive by many kinds of entertainers—

jugglers, acrobats, fire-eaters, stilt-walkers, animal-trainers with monkeys and bears, mummers and mime-artists, mimics, wrestlers and, most important of all, by ballad-singers and story-tellers. It is probable that, even in the Dark Ages, the wandering minstrel, with his songs and stories of heroes such as Beowulf, brought entertainment to those huddled round some hearth.

Yet the new dramatic tradition began with none of these performers. It grew up in the churches. We do not know all the reasons for this, but we can see that drama grew out of an extension of religious ceremony and ritual in a way that helped to make religious themes more vivid and easily understood by ordinary folk. We must remember that Greek theatre grew out of ritual worship of the god Dionysus.

The Church doubtless found the emerging drama to be a useful method of religious instruction. However, as time went on it was unable to control the virile growth of the child which it had bred, and the maturing drama broke out of the confines of the church buildings and developed into a secular activity. Yet, even after ecclesiastical ties had been broken, drama kept its religious content. The great cycles of the Mystery plays continued to tell the enduring Old Testament stories, and to trace the nativity, life, crucifixion and resurrection of Christ, concluding with a representation on stage of the Last Judgement.

Let us now look in more detail at what happened.

In the church

Drama can be broken down into three main ingredients: (1) impersonation; (2) dialogue; and (3) action. Each follows from the other, and they probably evolved in Church drama in the following way.

(1) *Impersonation*
In a church service, when a priest begins the litany he makes a statement and the congregation reply. Perhaps the choir may sing an anthem, in the middle of which one of its number may sing a solo part representing the words of, say, one of the Apostles, or even Christ. In both of these cases, roles are being played, there is impersonation going on. In other words, the priest and congregation, choir and soloist are, in a sense, actors who are playing parts.

(2) *Dialogue*
The impersonation could be developed if there were to be two or more soloists, and they were to sing or say words to one another in such a way that a story was told. There is now only one element of total drama lacking, and that is action.

(3) *Action*
The priest and choristers could move from their fixed positions, and

begin to make the story more vivid by processing round the church or by actually acting out the story before the congregation.

The scenario outlined above did indeed occur in many English churches during the ninth, tenth and eleventh centuries. Phase (3), action, probably followed because the words were in Latin. The acting out, or rather miming, of the story would help the people (who could by now almost be called an audience) to understand what was going on.

In early English church festivals, there were sung sections known as *tropes*. Again, these developed in rather the same way as the dithyrambic hymn in ancient Greek religion (originally a song of praise of the god Dionysius, it gradually took on a narrative, dramatic form). These *tropes* developed into very short Latin playlets. The earliest playlet which we have on record was the Easter *trope*, which possibly dates from as early as the ninth century. The three Marys, played by choirboys or priests, approach another priest dressed in a white robe who is impersonating the angel at the tomb of Jesus. '*Quem quaeritis*?' he intones. The entire play contains only four lines of dialogue:

> *Quem quaeritis in sepulchro, o Christicolae?*
> (Whom seek ye in the tomb, O Christian women?)

The women reply

> *Iesum Nazarenum crucifixum, o caelicola.*
> (Jesus of Nazareth Who was crucified, O heavenly one)

The angel declares

> *Non est hic: surrexit sicut praedixerat.*
> *Ite, nuntiate quia surrexit de sepulchro.*
> (He is not here: He has arisen just as he predicted.
> Go, announce that he has arisen from the tomb)

The angel holds up a linen shroud to show the women that He is gone. The church bells then ring out, and the audience sing the *Te Deum*.

Somewhere, one Easter-tide, a little scene was added which is not to be found in the Gospel story. Somebody with imagination—a priest, monk or layman—decided to write an episode showing the three Marys stopping to buy spices at a market-stall. At first, the stall-holder was merely a non-speaking part. In later versions of the episode he is given words, and he bargains with the women. Later still, he is shown trying to cheat them. Finally he becomes a comic figure, who would be received with immediate laughter.

Did the ordinary folk watching the play know that this scene was not in the Bible? It is hard to say. At any rate, they felt no inhibition about laughter in church: it did not conflict with their reverence for holy things. Other episodes appeared which were not drawn directly from the Bible. For instance, there was one play about St Nicolas (Santa Claus), who was becoming a very popular saint.

Outside the church

The plays became increasingly elaborate in terms of the number of scenes, actors involved and settings. Sometimes different acting areas or little stages were set up round the church. Soon it became impossible to cope with the requirements of performing a sequence of plays inside a church, and a move was made out into the churchyard.

Little is known about the staging arrangements. Possibly the audience surrounded the actors, or perhaps the action was set up against the west door or a wall of the church. It is probable that, in order to make the plays more accessible to ordinary folk, English dialogue now replaced Latin.

A part of a manuscript of a play called *Adam* has come down to us, containing stage directions which give some idea as to how the plays of this period were presented. It belongs to the twelfth or thirteenth century. The opening stage direction dictates:

> A Paradise is to be made in a raised spot, with curtains and cloths of silk hung round it at such a height that the persons in the Paradise may be visible from the shoulders upwards. Fragrant flowers and leaves are to be set round about, and divers trees put therein with hanging fruit, so as to give the likeness of a most delicious spot.

Later in the play the manuscript requires that

> Adam and Eve walk about Paradise in honest delight. Meanwhile, the demons are to run about the stage with suitable gestures, approaching Paradise from time to time and pointing out the forbidden fruit to Eve as though persuading her to eat it.

At the end of the play, there is the following direction:

> Then shall come the Devil and three or four devils with him, carrying in their hands chains and iron fetters which they shall put upon the necks of Adam and Eve. And some shall pull, and others push them to Hell; and hard by Hell shall be other devils ready to meet them, who shall hold high revel at their fall. And certain other devils shall point them out as they come, and shall snatch them up and carry them into Hell; and there shall they make a great smoke arise, and call aloud to each other with glee in their Hell, and clash their pots and kettles that they may be heard without. And after a little delay the devils shall come out and run about the stage. But some shall remain in Hell.

Overcrowding was certainly not the only reason why the plays were no longer performed in churches. The parts traditionally played by priests and other clergy were gradually being taken over by laymen, and the Church authorities may not totally have approved of this process. Nor may they have liked all the non-biblical additions and comic touches which now embellished the pure biblical stories.

The first outdoor performances probably occurred around AD 1200; and once freed from the constrictions of a building, the scope of the plays appears to have expanded rapidly. Soon the churchyard itself may not have been big enough—or perhaps the Church authorities now wanted plays removed altogether from church ground. By around AD 1300 performances began to move to the nearest available large space —the market-place or town square.

As the tradition became established over the years, another scene was added: the two disciples Peter and John were shown running to the tomb. Then a scene was incorporated showing Mary Magdalene meeting the risen Christ and mistaking him for the gardener. And so on, until incident after incident recorded in the Bible was dramatised.

At the same time, another development was taking place: vernacular (that is, words in the native language) was introduced into the middle of the Latin verse. In the end, the Latin was squeezed out, and plays of substantial length, sung wholly in the vernacular, were sung in church. Another development was happening at the same time as the others: gradually sections of the spoken word crept in, until the music was used only at selected moments in the drama.

By the eleventh century, drama of this kind was well established, and it continued to flourish for over two hundred years. After Easter, which was then the most important festival in the Church calendar, Christmas was second in significance as a festival. Nativity plays became popular, as they still are today in churches and schools up and down the country. A play called *The Three Kings* showed the anger of Herod when the Wise Men fail to return to see him after visiting the baby Jesus. In one version of the play the stage direction says:

The play ends, with Herod taking a sword from a bystander and brandishing it in the air.

This piece of stage business was obviously popular, for it is retained in the later Mystery plays where Herod develops into a raging, shouting character, whom the audience view with both fear and laughter.

As more actors became necessary, laymen (that is, ordinary men who were not priests or members of the choir) took some parts, but no women were allowed to perform. That would have been considered not merely unseemly, but indecent. It is not until 1660 that female actresses first appeared in England.

In the market-place

In the market square the same acting areas could be used as in the church, but it was now possible to make settings far more elaborate. God could be given a high stage to Himself, an ark could be built for Noah, a live ram used for the Abraham and Isaac play, and so on. The New Testament stories could reach a climax with Christ crucified on a cross raised high on an imaginary hill of Golgotha. The favourite and most spectacular piece of scenery was a Hell-mouth in the shape of the enormous head of a dragon or other monster, which sometimes could even be made to belch smoke. Out of this the Devil and his henchmen would come and go, both frightening and amusing the audience.

Eventually a whole cycle of plays was developed, which might take one or more days to perform. Because there was so much to be done in order to stage all the plays, for practical reasons different plays were allocated to different sections of the community. The strongest sense of affiliation in the medieval community was that created by the different trade guilds. These guilds were not much like modern trade unions, but were more like professional fellowships which watched over the welfare of a trade or craft as a whole, and encouraged professional pride among its member-tradesmen and craftsmen. Different trades also tended to live together in their own quarter of a town, and this assisted in the co-operation necessary to produce a play among themselves.

A guild would often be responsible for producing a play appropriate to its trade. For instance, the Grocers, who tempted with rich food, might produce *Adam and Eve*; Shipwrights or Water-carriers, *Noah's Ark*; Bakers, *The Last Supper*; Butchers *The Crucifixion*; and so on.

Thus developed the great cycles of English plays known as Mystery or Miracle plays. How the latter name arose is clear: some plays dealt with the miracles of Christ. Mystery comes from the French word *mystère*, which was used in the Middle Ages to describe any trade or craft. Thus, Mysteries came to refer to the plays produced by the trade guilds.

Manuscripts have survived of forty-eight plays which were performed in York, thirty-two in Wakefield (which is also called the Towneley cycle), twenty-four in Chester, and a few of those which were put on in Coventry. There is also a manuscript which bears the name 'N' town. There are various claims that these plays belong to Northampton, Lincoln or elsewhere; or that they were designed to be performed in any town, the 'N' to be filled in with the name of the town, as appropriate.

As well as some texts of the plays, financial accounts which shed light on many other details of the productions have come down to us:

they list items such as timber, paint, angels' wigs made of cloth, the archangel Gabriel's wings, flowers for paradise, '2 coats and a pair of hosen for Eve, stained', 'A coat and hosen for Adam, stained' and 'A face [mask] for the Father [God]'. The Trinity House guild of master-mariners and pilots in Hull performed a *Noah* pageant on Plough Monday, 1483, and list among their expenses:

> To the minstrels, 6d.
> To Noah and his wife, 1s 6d.
> To Robert Brown playing God, 6d

It seems that not all were, strictly speaking, amateurs. To add to the cost it sometimes fell to the organisers to provide a considerable quantity of food and drink during the rehearsal period!

Mystery plays were not confined to England, but evolved and blossomed during the Middle Ages all over Europe, especially in Germany, France and the Low Countries.

We do not know of all the places where Mysteries of some sort were performed, and many plays have been lost; for example, the Passion Play of London and southern England. However, we do know that plays were staged between the 1260s and 1580s at, among other places, Coventry, York, Chester, Wakefield, Wymondham, Norwich, Newcastle, Bristol, Beverley, Hull, Manningtree, Tewkesbury, in Cornwall and almost certainly at Lincoln.

The Pageants

In 1264 Pope Urban IV instituted the festival of Corpus Christi, to be held each year on the Thursday after Trinity Sunday. On this June day in early summer, when the weather was often warm, it was the custom of the craft and trade guilds to walk in holiday procession through the streets. Gradually, there grew a tradition that in the course of the procession each guild represented should present their biblical play.

The problem of how to make the plays 'mobile' was solved by performing them on a cart, which was probably wreathed with greenery and decorated for the occasion, rather like a modern carnival float. The carts would have been quite high off the ground, so that the crowd of spectators had a clear view. The space under the cart could also have been hung round with curtains and used as a changing-room for the actors. These carts were called 'pageants', and in time the sequence of plays performed upon them also became known as pageants. Guild competed with guild to provide the most magnificent pageant. Each show cost an estimated fifteen pounds (which must be multiplied by at least two hundred times to arrive at the modern equivalent).

There is so much that we do not know, such as whether the mobile pageant replaced the static religious drama in the market-place, or whether the two traditions continued side by side. We have only a vague idea how the pageants and other essential properties looked. Music may have played a significant part in the productions.

The best way to see the cycle of pageant plays was to get out of bed early on the morning of the feast of Corpus Christi (or at Whitsun, if in Chester), pack up enough food for the day and go out into the streets. If you were lucky, you would be in time to gain a good vantage-place overlooking one of the 'stations', which were so called because they were locations on the route of the procession where each pageant cart would stop and give a performance of its play before moving on. Thus, without moving from your position in the street, each play in turn would come to you. We have a record of the exact location of each station used in the York pageant.

Before the end of the thirteenth century the 'secularisation' of drama was almost complete. The Church had ceased to sponsor the plays. The town councils now organised the pageants and, while keen to keep the religious basis of the stories, they were eager to please their townsfolk by retaining the elements which each year went down well with the audience.

And that audience wanted to see themes in the plays which reflected their everyday lives. Religion was ever-present; but so were hard task-masters, nagging wives, winter cold and hunger, summer heat and harvest, rogues and thieves.

The Second Shepherds' Play in the Wakefield cycle developed to such an extent that only the last few minutes of a three-quarter-hour play are to do with the biblical story of the angel appearing to shepherds in the fields, and their visit to the stable to worship the baby Jesus. Even in that episode, the shepherds depart from the Gospel account by giving to the baby presents of a bunch of cherries, a bird—and a tennis ball!

The main part of the play tells how three shepherds manage to detect a sheep-thief called Mak. They grumble along the way about their wives and the weather, and show their annoyance at the shabby treatment which hired men often received at the hands of their masters. These themes are put over with a freshness and humour which are typical of the Mystery plays as a whole. The drama was young, irrepressibly exuberant and vigorous, and using a language that was rapidly changing and expanding.

There is no attempt in the play to convey any historical sense of Palestine at the time of the birth of Christ. The appearance of the angel and the visit to the manger seem almost tacked on to the end as an afterthought. The Church may have fretted about such developments, but it was, so to speak, no longer paying the piper, and so it could call the tune no longer.

It is this secularisation of drama which was to prove so important in its future development. The Fall of Adam and Eve, the murder of Abel by his brother Cain, the massacre of the innocent children by Herod— in Christian terms all these events are redeemed in Heaven, where the good have their reward. But in the Mystery plays which deal with these events, there is a frequent sense of sadness and waste which looks forward to the pathos and terror of Elizabethan and Jacobean tragedy. There was plenty of humour and wit in the Mystery plays; there was also a sense that man's life might not be a comedy with tragic interludes, but the reverse.

The great period of the Mystery plays was approximately 1350 to 1550, although they existed before and survived after these dates. In the sixteenth century, during the Reformation, attempts were made to suppress them; but they remained popular, especially in the north of England. The tradition of their performance gradually died out, and by the end of the sixteenth century they were virtually dead, replaced by tragedy and comedy based on non-religious material. It is an attractive idea to imagine that William Shakespeare, the greatest tragic and comic playwright of the new age (or, most would say, of any era), as a Warwickshire lad aged twenty-two, may have been present in Coventry when some of the last performances of the mystery plays were staged there in 1586.

In modern times there have been several revivals of Mystery plays in York and Lincoln, among other places. However, nothing like the length and splendour of the originals has been attempted, performances being limited to three hours on a static set. The sight and sound of pageants carts adorned in their former glory and rumbling again through the streets would be wonderful. Even sophisticated inhabitants of the video age would stop and stare, just like our ancestors did six hundred years ago.

Morality plays

Background

Morality plays flourished between about AD 1400 and 1500, thus coinciding with the slow passing away of the Middle Ages. Whereas Mystery plays dealt with the lives and actions of biblical or saintly characters, Morality plays concerned themselves with the problems of ordinary men. To emphasise this, the main character was often given a name such as 'Mankind' or 'Everyman'. The plays show the gradual movement of drama away from the influence of the Church, and its increasing use as entertainment. However, in Moralities the aim to teach a moral point is still present, as, of course, their name itself suggests. Instead of taking stories from the Bible, the playwrights made them up. Each play was complete, and did not form part of a cycle, unlike the Mystery plays.

The story of a Morality play took the form of an allegory, a device that has always been popular and of which medieval man was particularly fond. Allegory is the telling of a simple story which has another meaning under the surface. In Langland's allegorical poem *Piers Plowman* (?1375), Truth (God), Wrong (the Devil), a lady called Holy Church, Liar, Reason, Conscience and others appear in a story with a moral meaning. During the 1590s the poet Edmund Spenser (?1552–99) published a long poem called *The Faerie Queene* (allegorical name for Queen Elizabeth I), in which twelve knights represent twelve important virtues. The most famous of all allegories is probably John Bunyan's *Pilgrim's Progress* (1678). On the literal level, this is about a man called Christian who leaves his home and travels towards the Heavenly City. Allegorically, it is clear that Christian represents any Christian soul—as Everyman stands for all men in *Everyman*—and that the Vices and Virtues which beset him are common to all.

A typical story in a Morality play concerned a man who is surrounded by temptations. These temptations were not just in his mind, but were actually characters on the stage, who talked to the man and tried to persuade him to abandon his good way of living. This group of characters were known as Vices, and had names such as Mischief, Ignorance, Pride, Avarice, Anger, Envy, Covetousness, Gluttony, Sloth (the last seven being the names of the Seven Deadly Sins). In one play there was a fast-living lady of the town called Abominable Living!

However, the Vices did not have it all their own way. Ranged against them were a group of good characters who tried to encourage Man to continue to live a good life. Their names were Virtues, such as Charity, Mercy, Conscience, Perseverance, Hope.

During the course of the play the Vices and Virtues struggle to gain Man's attention. The group which wins will gain a great prize: Man's soul. The Virtues are usually represented as elderly men, wise and sober; the Vices are young men dressed in the height of fashion. Usually Man gives in to the temptations of the Vices for a while, and lives a riotous life. As time passes and he grows old, Man becomes troubled as to how his account stands with God, and the Virtues again begin to exert some influence over him. Usually, Man repents of his sins before Death comes to carry him off, and he is allowed to enter Heaven and be with God.

The outline above makes a typical Morality play sound like a rather dull sermon. Yet in performance it could be lively and absorbing. Although the naming of most of the characters after a single aspect of human nature does tend to restrict any interesting development of individuality, nevertheless they are not merely symbolic, despite their abstract names, and we are seeing the beginnings of a variety of dramatic types which were to be developed one hundred years or so later in the Elizabethan theatre.

The appearance of Death on stage, coming to claim the body of Man when his time on earth was up, would have struck fear into the heart of the medieval audience. It was believed that supernatural powers could actually take on physical shape. In those days, people could die young of many things which can now be cured by an injection or a course of pills, and you would have been lucky to reach the age of forty or fifty. As a result, even healthy people were aware that Death might tap them on the shoulder at any time.

In one play of the period a citizen of London is walking along with his wife and servant when Death meets them. The wife deserts her husband and the servant runs away, leaving the citizen to face Death alone. He prays to Death and tries to bribe him to go away. But Death is quite determined: the man's hour has come, so he must leave his wife and children, and abandon his business no matter what state it is in. 'For,' says Death, holding up an arrow in his hand,

I have commission to strike you with this black dart called pestilence [that is, the plague or Black Death]; my master [that is, God] hath so commanded me: and as for gold, I take no thought of it, I love it not; no treasure can keep me back the twinkling of an eye from you; you are my subject, and I am your lord.

He then explains that the three arrows in his hand are Plague, Famine and War, and ends his speech with a terrifying warning which he probably addressed directly to the wide-eyed audience:

I overthrow the dancer, and stop the breath of the singer, and trip the runner in his race. I break wedlock, and make many widows. I do sit in judgment with the judge, and undo the life of the prisoner, and at length kill the judge also himself. I do summon the great bishops, and cut them through their robes. I utterly banish the beauty of all courtiers, and end the miseries of the poor. I will never leave off until all flesh be utterly destroyed. I am the greatest cross and scourge of God.

Sometimes the Devil himself, or one of his lieutenants, would appear, an event that was eagerly looked forward to by the audience. In one play called *Mankind* (?1475) some of the Vices actually go round amongst the audience taking a collection before the Devil appears. This is one of the clues that these plays were performed by actors who earned their living from acting, and who would not miss a chance to 'cash in' on a popular part of the performance.

Despite their moral tone, the plays show a more developed sense of humour than previous drama. This spirit grows in the Tudor Interludes, to reach maturity in Elizabethan comedy. In many ways, Morality plays link medieval with modern drama.

The performances

Anywhere where drama is performed can become a 'theatre'. However, we usually reserve the name for buildings which are put up with the express purpose of performing plays inside them. Morality plays were designed to be staged simply in town squares or in the great halls of gentry or noblemen. One exception to this is a play called *The Castle of Perseverance* (?1425), which demands elaborate performance and for which a kind of open-air theatre, probably constructed from earth and wood, was created.

The play was probably first performed somewhere in Lincolnshire, or maybe East Anglia. It was staged in a circular acting area surrounded by a mound and a ditch, and perhaps a fence, which it seems were intended to block the view of spectators who had not paid the admission charge. Round the edge of the central acting area or 'place' were five little booth-stages or 'scaffolds'. These were the homes of God (who lived in the scaffold built on the eastern side), Flesh (south), World (west), Belial, that is, the Devil (north) and Covetousness (north-east). In the centre of the place was the Castle of Perseverance itself. The play is long and complicated. Briefly, the hero is called Humanum Genus (Mankind), and he is tempted to give in to Covetousness. He is led by Confession and Penitence to the Castle of Perseverance, where he is defended by various Virtues against the attacks of the Vices. But he is tempted by Covetousness to leave the castle and gain some wealth before he dies. This he does, and enjoys money and the sins of the flesh for a while; but he meets Death, loses all his possessions which a boy takes away, and dies. His Soul goes to Hell, and appeals to Mercy; who passes his appeal on to God; who saves the Soul, thanks to the redemption of Christ. The play ends with a warning; indeed the whole moral purpose was to demonstrate the evil of Covetousness (the desire to accumulate worldly possessions).

The play is rather dull to read, but it would have been a lavish spectacular to watch. Some of the stage directions indicate that the costumes were very colourful:

> The four daughters shall be clad in mantles, Mercy in white, Righteousness in red altogether, Truth in sad green and Peace in black and they shall play in the place all together till they bring up the soul.

The remains of two of the kind of auditorium used for a play like *The Castle of Perseverance* can still be seen in Cornwall. One is the St Piran Round, near Perranporth, and the other is at St Just-in-Penwith. They are worth a visit if you are ever in that part of England.

The actors

One crucial feature of Morality plays is that they were not performed by amateurs, like the Mystery plays, but by professional groups, which toured around giving performances whenever a suitable occasion—such as a public holiday—presented itself, and whenever they could find a suitable auditorium. For most of the plays, little scenery was needed, and a company who possessed a short, compact play could move easily from one district to another in order to find new audiences for the same play.

Companies of strolling players consisted of four or five people. The actor in charge would have played the main part, and he arranged the performance in much the same way as a modern theatre director. One of the actors was a boy with an unbroken voice, who could act the female parts. The remaining members of the troupe divided the parts amongst themselves.

An episode has survived from an anonymous play called *Sir Thomas More* (1595), about the great Tudor statesman who was Chancellor of England for (and was eventually executed by) King Henry VIII, who reigned from 1509 to 1548. Sir Thomas More (1478–1535) owned a splendid house in Chelsea, and in the play he has invited the Lord Mayor of London, the Aldermen of the City and all their ladies to a banquet. The feast is spread, the house is humming with the last-minute preparations of the servants, and More, as host, is checking that all is as it should be—when a travelling player arrives. In the extract below, the reference to the Lord Cardinal's Players shows that by this time (about 1525) great men were beginning to patronise companies of actors, subsidising them financially in the same way as the modern Arts Council of Great Britain subsidises artistic enterprise, and expecting them to perform for them at important occasions.

MORE: Welcome, good friend; what is your will with me?
PLAYER: My lord, my fellows and myself
   Are come to tender you our willing service,
   So please you to command us.
MORE: What! for a play, you mean?
   Whom do ye serve?
PLAYER: My Lord Cardinal's grace.
MORE: My Lord Cardinal's Players! Now, trust me, welcome!
   You happen hither in lucky time,

To pleasure me, and benefit yourselves.
The Mayor of London and some Aldermen,
His lady and their wives, are my kind guests
This night at supper. Now, to have a play
Before the banquet will be excellent.
I prithee, tell me, what plays have ye?

The player runs through his repertoire, until he mentions a play called *The Marriage of Wit and Wisdom*, whereupon Sir Thomas More cries 'That, my lads, I'll none but that! The theme is very good.' He turns quickly to a servant who is standing nearby, and says:

Go, make him drink, and all his fellows too.
How many are ye?
PLAYER: Four men and a boy.
MORE: But one boy? Then I see,
There's but few women in the play.
PLAYER: Three, my lord; Dame Science, Lady Vanity,
And Wisdom—she herself.
MORE: And one boy to play them all? By'r Lady, he's loaden!
Well, my good fellows, get ye straight together,
And make ye ready with what haste ye may.

But the performance is delayed while one of the players runs to the next village to fetch a beard for young Wit. More immediately steps into the breach and plays the part of Wit himself. After the play, the actors are paid and given supper and lodging for the night.

This episode, although not written until the end of the sixteenth century, presents a vivid picture of the circumstances under which strolling players had been performing for a century and more previously.

Groups of travelling players still exist, and there is one company called The Medieval Players which tours around Britain performing plays like the one that Sir Thomas More is supposed to have seen and taken part in. They perform wherever they can find a suitable hall or space and even act out their plays in the street. Apart from their modern transport, their lifestyle is similar to that of their forerunners five hundred years ago.

Tudor Interludes

Background

The five Tudor kings and queens, from Henry VII to Elizabeth I, sat on the throne of England between 1485 and 1603, and it is during the middle of this period that 'Interludes' were popular.

There is uncertainty as to what the word 'interlude' means. It comes from the Latin *interludium* which means 'play-between'. Possible meanings are:

A play acted out between two or more actors.
A play performed between two courses of a meal, or between the evening meal and bedtime.
A light-hearted play performed between two more serious 'morality' plays.

Whatever the word means, the subject-matter of 'Interludes' is a development from the Morality plays. Probably the audiences were becoming dissatisfied with characters and themes which were to do with religion, or which merely demonstrated moral virtues and vices. Now spectators were becoming eager for plays which depicted the tragedies and comedies of individuals, either great people whose doings they might hear about, or ordinary people such as they might see every day in the streets.

Some Interludes still made a serious moral point, and were adaptations from Morality plays. Among these may be counted *Nature* (?1495) and *Fulgens and Lucrece* (?1496), both by Henry Medwall (1462–?1505); *Magnificence* (?1515—possibly seen by King Henry VIII) by John Skelton (?1460–1529); and *The Interlude of the Four Elements* (?1517) and *Calisto and Melebea* (?1527), both of which may have been written by John Rastell (1475–1536), and both pointing out the moral importance of education.

Other Interludes lost their religious point and were intended as pure entertainment. The best plays of this type were those of John Heywood (?1497–?1580), which included *The Four P's* (?1520), a competition between four characters as to who can tell the biggest lie. The winner claims that he never saw a woman in a temper. *John John* (?1520) (which is the short title normally given to the play) is the humorous story of a hen-pecked husband who thinks that his wife is unfaithful to him, and suspects that she is gadding about with the village priest. The nagging wife and the brow-beaten husband are frequently seen as figures of fun on the English stage (poor Noah suffered from the same problem in the Mystery plays, and in 1594 William Shakespeare (1564–1616) was to suggest how to deal with a troublesome wife in *The Taming of the Shrew*).

Thus, the Tudor Interludes are a vital link between medieval drama and the rich, varied stories and characters to be found in the Elizabethan drama written after the 1580s.

The actors

They travelling acting troupes who performed Interludes were much the same as those which staged the old Morality plays; but as the sixteenth century progressed these companies became increasingly well organised.

They travelled from place to place in some kind of covered wagon, in which they carried all their costumes and stage properties, and also trestles and boards which could be speedily arranged to form a stage (to 'tread the boards' is an expression which is still used to describe the business of acting). They carted about hardly any scenery. A curtain to be hung at the rear of the stage served as a backdrop through which the actors could enter and exit. Items such as flags or shields had to suffice in order to create a quick sense of place or character.

The performances

There were three kinds of place where a company might seek to perform. First, they could go to a fairground and set up their stage. This, however, was an unreliable business: although a collection could be taken among the spectators who might drift along to watch, it was difficult to force them to pay even if they had watched the whole play. Remember that these travelling players were all professionals, and had to make a living.

A second possibility was to go to an inn and find out whether the landlord was prepared to give permission for the company to set up their stage in the inn yard. It must have occurred to the landlord that both he and the actors could profit under such an arrangement. By allowing the players to perform their play, he provided entertainment for guests who were staying at the inn, and attracted more customers, who paid, say, one penny at the door to the players as an admission charge to see the play, and then probably purchased his ale. These people, who were mainly craftsmen, apprentices or workmen, stood around the stage in the inn yard. The landlord's more important, richer guests avoided contamination by the sweaty crowd by watching from the gallery which ran round above the courtyards of most inns of the period.

Everybody was happy. The guests and the local people had cheap entertainment; the landlord and the players gained financially. Indeed, what had been created was really a rather good 'theatre'; and the buildings which were later to be built around London specifically for play-acting owed much to the design of inn yards.

Doubtless, if the play was a great success, the landlord would engage the actors to perform for a second night, thus beginning what is now called a 'run' of performances. If he was feeling particularly generous, he might well provide them with free supper and ale, and allow them to sleep comfortably in the hayloft, or in front of the kitchen fire.

A third place where the actors were received was at the manor house of the local squire, or even at the hall or castle of a nearby nobleman. Entertainment was not easy to find, and a rich man was glad of the chance to divert himself, his family and any guests who were staying with him. William Shakespeare, in his play *Hamlet*, shows how the arrival of the travelling players at Elsinore Castle greatly raises the spirits of the depressed young prince; and Prince Hamlet demonstrates great respect for the actors and love of their profession. If you turn back to pages 17–18, you will read of the kindly way in which Sir Thomas More is reputed to have treated the players.

The main hall of a big house was the obvious place for the performance of a play, although we know very little of how such performances were organised. The actors probably looked at the playing space available and decided how to make the best use of it. Possibly the play was performed in front of the permanent wooden screen at the lower end of the hall. Many such screens survive today in big houses; and there are fine examples in some of the dining halls of the older Oxford and Cambridge colleges.

It was the upper classes who became the main patrons of actors, supporting them financially and in some ways fulfilling the same function as the Arts Council today. It is known that at the beginning of the sixteenth century the Lords Ferrers, Clinton, Oxford and Buckingham kept private actors. As the century wore on, increasing numbers of great men did so, the most famous being the Earl of Leicester, a favourite of Queen Elizabeth I. Plays were usually commissioned for special festive occasions, such as the celebration of a marriage, a birthday, Christmas or Twelfth Night. Guests were invited into the main hall for a feast laid on by the master of the house. The hall may have been packed not only with diners, table and chairs, but also with the servants of the house and retainers accompanying the guests; and an acting space had to be created in front of the screens for the players.

The household accounts of the Earl of Northumberland state that thirty-three shillings and four pence was spent in payment to visiting players during the Christmas holidays of 1511–12, and that twenty pence was the fee for each play. If you work out the sum (remembering that it is in old pre-decimal currency), it can be seen that a considerable number of plays were performed that Christmas at the Earl of Northumberland's house. In addition to payment, the actors would probably have received refreshment and lodging. If they were a travelling company, they would have packed up next morning and set off for the nearest town which might welcome them.

Not all places did so. Actors have always had the reputation of being unstable people, often regarded as little better than rogues or vagabonds. Accordingly, they would sometimes be refused entry to a town. The merchant classes in particular looked upon them as corrupting influences, likely to draw apprentices and working men away from their labours. The pleas of the actors that their plays were nearly always stories with a moral often fell on deaf ears.

Despite official disapproval, certain companies managed to establish bases at London inns. Edward Alleyn (1566–1626), a famous tragic actor, was at the Crosskeys in Gracechurch Street; and James Burbage (?–1597), head of Lord Leicester's company of players and father of the man for whom William Shakespeare was to write plays, was at the Bull, Bishopsgate.

It was not until 1572 that acting was recognised by royal decree as a lawful profession.

When permanent theatres began to be built in London from 1575 onwards, the merchants who ran the City allowed none to be built within the ancient walled area over which they had jurisdiction. Even today, until the building of the new Barbican complex, the Mermaid at Puddledock was the only theatre inside the city boundaries, and that was founded as recently as the 1960s; all the other theatres are in the West End of London or around and about.

There was one other place where interludes were performed: in academic institutions such as schools, universities and inns of court (that is, where lawyers are trained). *Gammer Gurton's Needle*, a farce about a lost needle which eventually turns up in one character's breeches (and a painful revelation it is!), was written in about 1552 by somebody whom we merely know from the title page as 'Mr S, Master of Art'. It is fairly certain that he was a fellow or scholar of Christ's College, Cambridge, for that is where his play was first performed.

Ralph Roister Doister, written about the same time by Nicholas Udall (?1505–56), headmaster of Westminster School (and former headmaster of Eton College), was almost certainly first performed by his pupils.

Tudor Interludes continued the movement away from religious plays, and represent the complete secularisation of drama in England which opened the way for the mature comedy and tragedy of the later Elizabethan era.

A note on the text

Everyman is sometimes dated as early as the reign of Edward IV (who reigned from 1471 to 1483), but around 1500 is the commonly accepted date. The play is one of the first to be printed in England, and there were at least four editions between 1510 and 1530, two printed by Richard Pynson and two by John Skot. After this, there is no known edition until the reprinting of Skot's edition of around 1529 by Thomas Hawkins in his *The Origins of English Drama, Volume 1* (Oxford, 1773). Since then there have been approximately one hundred and fifty editions. See Part 5 of these Notes for details of modern editions.

Part 2

Summaries
of EVERYMAN

A general summary

A Messenger comes forward to speak the prologue. He outlines the moral story which the audience is about to witness; and he introduces God, who, anguished at man's behaviour, has decided that He must call him to account. He commands Death, his 'mighty messenger', to go to Everyman and summon him to his final journey. Everyman is aghast that his day of reckoning is come and that nothing can delay it. He desperately appeals to Fellowship, Kindred and Cousin; each promises help, but each deserts him upon learning the nature of Everyman's journey. He next turns to his Goods, who points out that if he accompanies him it will be the worse for Everyman at his reckoning, and laughs at his distress. When he finally turns to his Good Deeds she is too weak to rise. She would go with him if she could, but he has given her too little nourishment during his life. Knowledge enters, and agrees to accompany him. After Everyman has whipped himself with the Scourge of Penance, Knowledge guides him to Confession, who shrives him from his guilt. Good Deeds becomes stronger, and is able to rise and accompany Everyman as he approaches the churchyard. Beauty, Strength, Discretion and Five Wits attend him for a while, but all are worldly attributes and shrink away from entering the grave with Everyman. Even Knowledge has to leave him at the end. As Good Deeds alone accompanies him into the grave, an Angel sings a welcome to his passing soul.

A learned Doctor comes forward and emphasises the moral meaning of the play.

Detailed summaries

The text of *Everyman* is continuous, and is not divided into acts and scenes. In order to facilitate reference to the Notes and Glossaries, the detailed summaries have been divided into ten sections. Broadly speaking, a new section begins at the entrances or exits which mark a new phase in the play.

There are 921 lines in the play, and references are the same in all editions.

Lines 1–79

A Messenger appears, acting as prologue. He tells the audience that they are about to witness a moral play entitled *The Summoning of Everyman*, which will illustrate how a man's life quickly passes away; how sin, which appeals to a man in his early years, causes distress to his soul when his body is buried in the earth; how Fellowship, Jollity, Strength, Pleasure and Beauty all fade 'as flower in May'; and how God calls upon every man to account for his life on earth. The Messenger then introduces God, warning the audience to listen carefully to what he says.

God, speaking from his throne, says that He perceives that mankind is 'Drowned in sin' and fails to acknowledge Him as God. Despite His death upon the Cross on behalf of mankind, God's law is ignored and man's mind is all upon worldly riches, pleasure and the seven deadly sins. The more God spares man from punishment, the worse he becomes; if He leaves man much longer to his own devices, he will come to be worse than the animals. Man is envious, forgetting all spirit of generosity. God decides that He must quickly call man to account. He had hoped that every soul would go to Heaven; but He sees that some traitors reject the bliss that He intended for them, that they are not grateful for the gift of life which He has lent them, and that they must be weeded out. Few pray to Him for the abundance of mercy that He has promised. Most are so weighed down with worldly riches that God must execute His Justice upon them.

Accordingly, God summons Death, who enters. He commands Death to go to Everyman and inform him that he must immediately depart upon that pilgrimage to the grave which no man may escape. Death says that he will strike with his dart 'Everyman . . . that liveth beastly'.

NOTES AND GLOSSARY:

Messenger:	there is no prologue to the Dutch *Elckerlijc*, of which *Everyman* is presumed to be a translation. In view of the inaccuracies (Jollity and Pleasure do not appear in the play), it is likely that the prologue is not the work of the original translator. There are prologues in several other Morality Plays, three of them spoken by one called Messenger
give your audience:	pay attention
By figure:	in the form of
all day:	always
matter:	content
intent:	message, didactic purpose. The intention of the

	play is to warn that holy dying is difficult without holy living; thus, the moral must be heeded by all the audience, the young as well as the old
gracious:	devout, full of divine grace
bear away:	take away (and think about after the performance)
Man, in the beginning...:	see Ecclesiasticus 7:36: 'Whatsoever thou takest in hand, remember the end, and thou shalt never do amiss.' The same proverb is used in various forms in three other Moralities
God speaketh:	God probably spoke from a raised structure situated on or near the stage so that, as with some of the Mystery plays, he was seen to be manifestly superior to the other characters. His speech, lamenting man's sin and ingratitude, featured in Mystery plays such as *Noah*
unkind:	undutiful, ungrateful
ghostly sight:	spiritual vision
when I for them died:	God is referring to Himself as Christ, when He was made man and died for mankind
suffered to be dead:	allowed myself to be killed
healed their feet:	an allusion to Christ washing the feet of his disciples (see the Bible, John 13:1–20)
seven deadly sins:	in addition to the four mentioned, they are envy, sloth and gluttony
As:	with the result that
covetise:	covetousness, avarice
Every man:	in various texts the term Everyman/everyman appears with or without capital letters. It is probably intended that God's speech should sound ambiguous, so that He is finding fault both with the character of Everyman (who is clearly referred to for the first time in line 66) and with every member of the audience
be nothing sure:	are by no means certain
forbear:	spare
appaireth:	deteriorates, degenerates, decays
reckoning:	accounting, as in the checking of an account-book
and:	if
tempests:	riotous behaviour
mansion:	natural dwelling and final resting place
deject:	base, abject
needs:	of necessity
pilgrimage:	the idea of the journey from life to death as a pilgrimage is common in the Middle Ages, and is

	used as late as 1678 in *Pilgrim's Progress* by John Bunyan
in no wise:	in no way, by no method
tarrying:	delaying
overall:	everywhere
cruelly:	unrelentingly, without pity
beset:	set about, attack
Out of:	outside
richesse:	wealth, riches
depart:	separate (him)
Except that:	Unless

Lines 80–205

Everyman enters. Death knows that Everyman's mind is on worldly matters, and that he little thinks that Death is coming. He tells Everyman of the journey upon which he must go, and how he must take along his account-book in order to present before God the list of his 'many bad deeds, and good but a few'. Everyman cries that he is not ready for a reckoning before God, and offers Death a thousand pounds if he will go away and come again in twelve years' time, when he, Everyman, will have amended his life. Death replies that he cares nothing for money or the importance of individuals, and that weeping and praying will not hold him back: Death sooner or later comes to all men. He confirms that this is a pilgrimage from which no man returns. Everyman asks whether he will have company on his pilgrimage, and Death replies that he may—if he can find anyone prepared to go with him. Death expresses astonishment that a man with his five wits about him did not understand that his life has only been lent to him, and that Death may come at any time to take that life away and pass it on to another person. Everyman begs to be spared until the next day, but Death declares that, for Everyman, today 'is the day/That no man living may scape away'. Warning Everyman to prepare himself, Death departs.

Everyman curses the day that he was born, for he fears that nobody will accompany him on his journey, and he knows that his reckoning with God is so poor that he risks the agony of eternal damnation. He must do something quickly. He cries to God, the creator of all things, for help. He decides to speak to his old friend Fellowship: they have had such jolly times together that he will surely go with Everyman on his journey. Fellowship enters, and Everyman greets him heartily.

NOTES AND GLOSSARY:

endure:	suffer
forget:	forgotten

Wouldest thou wit?: Would you like to know?

the heavenly sphere: it was believed that the earth was the centre of the universe, around which were a series of crystal spheres upon which were fixed the moon, planets, sun and stars. God dwelt in a fixed heaven of pure light in the outer sphere

reckoning: rendering of accounts

This blind matter . . . wit: This strange business disturbs my mind

thy book of count: Death tells Everyman that he must render his list of good and bad deeds to God in the manner of a bailiff rendering accounts to his lord

turn gain: return

wise: fashion, way of living

Have ado . . . way: let us get going on that journey

make none attorney: appoint nobody to stand in your place

that no man dreadeth: who fears nobody

rest: arrest

O Death, thou comest . . . in mind: see the Bible, Matthew 24:50–1

good: goods, wealth

set not: set no store, am not influenced

and I would receive: if I was prepared to accept

'Death giveth no warning': a popular proverb which was constantly emphasised by medieval preachers

But twelve year . . . abiding: if I could stay alive for just another twelve years

clear: free of blemish

haste thee lightly . . . gone: hurry off quickly on

prove: test, make trial of

the tide abideth no man: another popular proverb, usually rendered today as 'time and tide wait for no man'

of nature: of necessity, in the course of nature

for saint charity: in the name of holy charity

Hie thee that thou were gone: hurry up and go

weenest thou: do you think, suppose

wend: thought, supposed

go: gone, dead

go therefro: leave it, go from it, pass on

wits: senses. The Church taught that the five senses could be put to either good or bad use

For: in case

wretched caitiff: miserable villain. Everyman is addressing himself

gentle: noble, gracious

good advisement: due consideration, fair warning

keep: protect, guard

my writing:	the preparation of my account
be get:	been born
be:	been
ago:	gone
and I:	if I were to go
affiance:	trust

Lines 206–318

Fellowship immediately sees that Everyman is depressed, and declares that he will help Everyman, standing by him to the death. He will even go with Everyman to Hell. Everyman says that if he were to trust Fellowship and was then to be deserted, he would 'ten times sorrier be'. Fellowship grandly boasts that his words are followed by actions.

Accordingly, Everyman tells him of the dangerous journey that he has been commanded to undertake in order to render his account before God. Fellowship suddenly cools in his eagerness to stand by Everyman, for he fears that such a journey would bring him pain. An anguished Everyman protests that Fellowship promised to go with him; but when Fellowship hears that Death was the messenger who brought Everyman the news of the journey and that there will be no returning, he has no hesitation in going back upon his word. He will indulge with Everyman in food, drink and women—even murder—but he 'will not a foot with thee go' upon Everyman's inevitable journey. Everyman, seeing that Fellowship's mind is all on pleasure, and that no appeal to their long friendship will prevail, bids him farewell, and Fellowship departs hurriedly.

Everyman does not know where to turn now for help, and understands the truth of the proverb 'In prosperity men friends may find,/ Which in adversity be full unkind'. He decides to appeal to the members of his family.

NOTES AND GLOSSARY:

gramercy:	thank you
break:	open, reveal
a good friend at need:	a variation of the proverb 'A friend in need is a friend indeed'. Compare with line 854
deserve:	repay
strait count:	precise account
Adonai:	a Hebrew name for God
Promise is duty:	proverbial. Compare with line 821, where the more usual form 'promise is debt' occurs
take counsel:	talk it over
fear:	frighten
quick:	alive

bought:	redeemed (a reference to Christ's redemption of mankind through his own death)
For no man . . . not go:	the double negative is a frequent and acceptable form of emphasis in medieval literature
loath:	loathsome, hateful
pardie:	by God
haunt to women . . . company:	spend time in the delightful company of women
while the day is clear:	either (1) until daybreak, or (2) while things go well. Probably both meanings are intended
will not that way:	will not go/do not wish to go that way (a verb of motion is often omitted)
simple:	foolish
take the labour . . . saint charity:	take the trouble to escort me at the beginning of my way, for the sake of holy charity. Compare with line 675
a new gown:	a splendid gown was a sign of wealth
tarried:	stayed
speed:	protect, assist, watch over
fay:	faith
betake:	bequeath, entrust, commend
parting is mourning:	based on the proverb 'Sorrow is at parting if laughter be at meeting'. Compare with William Shakespeare's *Romeo and Juliet* (?1596), II.2.184: 'parting is such sweet sorrow'
depart:	part
Ah, Lady, help!:	in his distress, Everyman calls on the Virgin Mary, Mother of Christ, to help him
'In prosperity . . . unkind':	a proverb
Sith:	since
'kind will creep . . . go':	a proverb, implying that whatever the difficulties kinsmen will help one another
say:	assay, essay, try

Lines 319–377

Kindred and Cousin enter. They make the same declarations of love and support as Fellowship, insisting that a man may presume upon his kin for help. Everyman tells them of his journey, and how he must account for his many ill deeds and few good ones. When they hear this, Kindred and Cousin both refuse to accompany Everyman. Kindred says that Everyman can take his (her?) maid with him, but he himself will stay firmly behind. Kindred departs. Cousin, protesting that he must look to his own 'unready reckoning', also hurries away.

Everyman sadly laments the faithlessness of men, and how easily they break their promises.

NOTES AND GLOSSARY:

Cousin: used to denote any form of family kinship, not merely the relationship implied in modern usage

show us ... spare: tell us whatever is on your mind, and do not hold back

with you hold: stand by you, side with you

over his kin ... bold: a man may presume upon the support of his kinsman

hath me in wait: is lying in wait for me (referring to the Devil)

used: practised, committed

liefer ... water: prefer to fast on bread and water

bore: born

Ah ... merry man!: ah, sir, what a merry man you are!

Saint Anne: mother of the Virgin Mary

As for me: as far as I am concerned

so God me speed: as God may help me

I will deceive ... most need: this is in direct contrast with Knowledge's promise to Everyman in lines 522–3. In the anonymous morality play *The Castle of Perseverance*, Mundus (the World) says of Man that 'In his most need I shall him fail' (line 2698)

It availeth ... tice: it is no use trying to entice us

nice: wanton, promiscuous

abroad to start: to gad about

very effect: true intention

and I may: if I can

Lines 378–462

Since he has all his life loved riches, Everyman decides that he will appeal to his Goods, who comes forward from a corner where he has lain trussed up and piled high in chests and sacks. When Everyman tells him of his problem, Goods replies that he can only help in this world, and that if he goes on the journey it will count against Everyman: for, love of worldly treasure leads a man to his damnation. Also, worldly wealth is perishable, and cannot be removed. Goods is surprised at Everyman's notion that he owns Goods, who has been merely lent to him for a while. Goods destroys a man's soul and, when that man is dead, his Goods passes on to another man and deceives him in the same fashion. When Everyman curses him for his treachery, Goods laughs at him and departs.

NOTES AND GLOSSARY:

hereto:	to this
fair words ... fain:	a proverb
me of to provide:	to provide myself with
Good:	Goods, Property, Worldly Wealth
Lightly me say:	tell me quickly
of counsel ... desire thee:	I must ask for your advice
disease:	problem, difficulty, trouble
Jupiter:	strictly speaking, King of the Roman gods. Here used in the general sense of 'judge'
peradventure:	perhaps
ever among:	commonly, popularly
money maketh ...:	proverb
blind:	illegible, difficult to read
that hast thou for:	that has happened because of
that fearful answer:	that is, the rendering of his account before God
leasing:	a lie, lying
during:	during (your lifetime)
dolour:	distress
ware:	aware
all I may wite ...:	I can blame everything on having wasted my time
Weenest thou:	do you think, suppose
wend:	thought, supposed
condition:	nature, disposition
spill:	destroy, ruin
guise:	custom, practice
reprefe:	disgrace, shame
in care:	into a state of distress
Whereof:	of which
heartly:	sincere, heartfelt

Lines 463–521

Thinking of those in whom he has trusted and who have deserted him, Everyman is ashamed of himself. He begins to realise that he must look to his Good Deeds. However, she is so weak that she is unable to move or even speak. He calls to her. She feebly answers him from where she lies, cold in the ground. She would willingly accompany Everyman on his journey, but she is not strong enough to do so because he has not looked after her during his lifetime. She shows him his book of accounts, wherein Everyman cannot see recorded a single good deed. He asks what he can do. She says that, although she is unable to go with him, her sister, Knowledge, will stay by his side and help him to face 'that dreadful reckoning'.

NOTES AND GLOSSARY:

gone: go
come right well: be very welcome
And you do by me: if you will act by my advice
on you fall: happened to you
of all: for everything
eke: also
ever shall: ever shall be
Knowledge: suggesting here 'acknowledgement or recognition of sins'

Lines 522—669

Knowledge enters, and immediately confirms that she will go with Everyman and stay by his side, 'In thy most need to go by thy side'. Everyman gives thanks to God for this welcome help. Knowledge leads him to the House of Salvation in order to meet the holy man called Confession.

Confession appears, before whom Everyman kneels and asks for mercy from God. Confession shows him the Scourge of Penance, wherewith Everyman is to beat himself as a reminder of Christ's scourging. After that, Good Deeds will join him. He can be certain of mercy if he asks it of God. Everyman declares that he will willingly undergo the pain of this penance in order to gain such mercy, and he cries to God for forgiveness and to the Virgin Mary that she should intercede with her Son on his behalf. Whereupon he takes from Knowledge the Scourge of Penance and, baring his back, whips himself in order that, by suffering, he may escape the sharp fire of Purgatory.

To the delight of Everyman, Good Deeds now becomes strong enough to get up and go with him. Knowledge gives him the Garment of Contrition and explains that wearing it will make him more acceptable in the sight of God. Good Deeds tells him that he must also summon Discretion, Strength and Beauty to accompany him, and Knowledge points out that he also needs the advice of his Five Wits. Everyman calls upon them all to 'come hither and be present'.

NOTES AND GLOSSARY:

smart: pain, suffering
cognition: knowledge, direction
House of Salvation: that is, the church; probably represented on stage by a small house or 'mansion' which resembled a church building
in good conceit with: well thought of by, highly esteemed by
O glorious fountain . . . : compare with the Bible, Zechariah 13:1. Everyman's style of speech becomes more high-

flown and elegant as his spiritual condition improves

Redempt with heart . . . : redeemed with heartfelt . . .

Shrift, mother . . . : compare with lines 539–44. Confession and Shrift are the same, and thus there seems to be a blurring of gender. This is either a mistake, or the playwright intends applicability to both sexes

for: in response to

voider: remover

ere thou scape: before you escape

sicker: sure

draweth: draws near

doth him bind: punishes himself

oil of forgiveness: either (1) the oil used to annoint the dying in extreme unction, or (2) a general term for God's mercy, or (3) a reference to the legend of the Oil of Mercy, which told of Seth's attempts to obtain the oil for his old and dying father, Adam

lighted: lightened, illumined

knots: that is, the knots of the scourge, which will be painful within (spiritually) as well as physically

at will: according to your wishes

divine: divinity

in this presence: that is, in the presence of Knowledge and Confession

conduiter: conductor, leader

foundator: founder

enlumineth: illuminates

thereby: by means of these

Moses' table: the two tablets, or tables, of law which Moses was given by God on Mount Sinai were regarded by medieval theologans as symbols of baptism and penance

my enemy: the Devil

by mean of . . . his passion: by means of your intercession be a partaker of your Son's glory through His passion

space: opportunity

gay and fresh: finely and fashionably dressed (compare with the Morality play *Mankind*, line 119)

the water clear: compare with lines 536, 545

purgatory: 'Purgatory (*Latin* purgare, to make clean, to purify) in accordance with Catholic teaching is a place or condition of temporal punishment for those who, departing this life in God's grace, are not entirely free from venial faults, or have not fully paid the satisfaction due to their transgressions' (*Catholic Encyclopaedia*)

now I can walk and go: according to Catholic doctrine, a man's good deeds can only count towards his salvation if all his mortal sins are confessed and forgiven

preparate: prepared

in every stound: always, in any difficulty

this garment: at this point Everyman puts on the Garment of Contrition over his fine clothes. A symbolic change of clothing to indicate a change in spiritual condition occurs in several Morality plays, for example, *Mundus et Infans*, *Wisdom*, *Mankind*, *Hickscorner*

behove: benefit, advantage

before God ... miss: you may feel the lack of it when you come into God's presence

borrow: protect, release

heal: well-being, safety, salvation

hight: are called

Wits: senses

incontinent: at once

Lines 670–771

Enter Discretion, Strength, Five Wits and Beauty. They all agree to accompany Everyman on his pilgrimage. Everyman makes his last will and testament, giving half his goods to the poor and setting the other half aside as a restitution for his sins (see note on 'In queth' below). He does this, he says, in order to defy and escape the Devil. Knowledge advises Everyman to go at once to Priesthood and to receive from him the last sacrament. Five Wits talks to Everyman concerning the reverence due to a priest, who has God's authority to administer all the seven sacraments and to teach Holy Scripture, and is in all things the way by which a man can be redeemed and brought to God ('We be their sheep, and they shepherds be'—line 767). Priests, says Five Wits, are more important than the angels in heaven (for a note on Five Wits' homily see pages 43–4). Everyman exits to receive the sacrament and extreme unction from the priest. Knowledge qualifies Five Wits' comments by criticising sinful priests who make money out of their ecclesiastical activities or frequent the company of women. Five Wits trusts to God that they may find no such priests.

NOTES AND GLOSSARY:

Advise you: consider

lofed: praised
laud: praise
to my business: for my business
for sweet ne sour: in good times or in bad, come what may, for better or worse
unto: until
advise you: consider, turn the matter over in your mind
with a good advisement and deliberation: having carefully considered and reflected upon the matter
monition: warning
In queth: either (1) as a bequest—probably to his family—, or (2) as a restitution for improperly gained money, which might include that acquired through working on holy days, false oaths, false weights and measures, taking more than a service was worth, withholding wages, theft, tax evasion, non-payment of debts, and simply owning much and giving little to the poor
there: where
despite: defiance
To go quit . . . day: to be released from his power today and ever afterwards
Priesthood: probably the same actor who played Confession
wise: case
holy sacrament and ointment: that is, the Viaticum (final Eucharist) and Extreme Unction (in which the dying man in annointed with ointment or oil)
hie . . . ready were: hurry up and get ready
commission: authority
the least priest: the New Mermaid edition of the play in *Three Late Medieval Morality Plays*, edited by G.A. Lester, Benn, London, 1981 reads '*at* least'. This is a misprint
in the world being: alive in the world
cure: responsibility
Which God . . . great pain: compare with lines 751–3
Fain . . . body: I would dearly love to receive the holy sacrament
ghostly: spiritual
five words: the five words with which the bread was consecrated in the Roman Catholic mass were *Hoc est enim corpus meum* ('For this is my body')
The priest bindeth . . . heaven: this means that priests have the power to absolve ('unbind') a person of his sins, if the sinner truly repents; or he can confirm ('bind')

those sins. Thus a priest has great power over a man's destiny in this world and the next. See the Bible, Matthew 16:19 and 18:18

ministers: administers

thou were worthy: you would be worthy of it

But all only: except from

stead: place

it is so: that is, that they are above the angels

God their Saviour ... tell: Knowledge is referring to the sin of simony, the corrupt practice of selling ecclesiastical preferments, or dealing commercially with sacred things. See the Bible, the Acts of the Apostles, 8:18–24, where St Peter criticises a certain Simon for attempting to buy with money the gift of the Holy Spirit

tell: pay out

Their children ... fires: that is, priests have illegitimate children and thus break their vows of chastity

---

Lines 772–889

Everyman returns from receiving the last sacrament. He is carrying a crucifix, and he makes Strength, Discretion, Knowledge, Beauty, Five Wits and Good Deeds each touch the crucifix in turn. Strength, Discretion and Knowledge all say that they will not leave Everyman until his pilgrimage is completed. Everyman becomes weaker as they travel together towards his grave. Beauty, when she realises that they are to enter to grave of Everyman for evermore, deserts him. Strength, Discretion and Five Wits also leave him. Everyman now understands who are his real friends, and warns those who hear him (that is, the audience) to take good note of it. Good Deeds affirms that she will not forsake him, and Knowledge says that he will stay by him until the moment of his death. All earthly qualities are seen to be vanities which will abandon men in the end.

Everyman calls on God for mercy and commends his soul into His hands before disappearing with Good Deeds into the grave. Knowledge points out to the audience that Everyman has now suffered what we shall all endure, and that Good Deeds shall look after him.

NOTES AND GLOSSARY:

your alder speed: the helper of you all

rood: cross

there I would be: to where I wish to be

strong: arduous

you fro: from you

be as sure:	stand as steadfastly
Judas Maccabee:	a famous leader of the Jews and freedom fighter against the Syrians in 168BC. The Second Book of Maccabees is well known for its prayers for the dead—see the Bible, II Maccabees 12:45. See also I Maccabees 3
consume:	decay, decompose
more and less:	either (1) all of you, great people and little, or (2) completely. Possibly both meanings are intended
smother:	be suffocated
cross out all this:	cancel completely my promise to stay with you
I take my tap . . . gone:	this phrase has been explained in different ways, but its general meaning is 'Goodbye, I'm off!'
and thou:	if you
liketh:	pleases
space:	while
hie:	hurry
to-brast:	break
you to displease:	for displeasing you
wot:	know
She:	see note on page 52
everychone:	everyone
Death bloweth his blast:	Death is often pictured with a trumpet
keep:	attend
where ye shall come:	what will become of you
All earthly things is but vanity:	see the Bible, Ecclesiastes 12:8
Short our end . . . pain:	shorten our time of death and diminish our pain
day of doom:	according to Catholic doctrine, the day on which all souls, good and bad, are called upon to make their final reckoning before God. Before that, at the hour of each person's death, he has to face his individual judgment before God
***In manus tuas . . . meum*:**	'Into thy hands, most mighty one, I commend my spirit for ever.' These are the last words spoken by Jesus on the cross (see the Bible, Luke 23:46)

Lines 890–921

An angel enters, and announces that the soul of Everyman has been welcomed into the kingdom of heaven, into which all who live well shall come before Judgment Day.

A learned Doctor comes forward and underlines the moral meaning of the play. He warns the audience that Pride deceives you in the end, and that Beauty, Five Wits, Strength and Discretion will forsake you. Only a man's Good Deeds stand by him, but even they have little power before God if they are too small. No man can make amends for his life after he is dead, for by then Mercy and Pity will have left him. If his reckoning is blotted, then God will cast him into eternal hellfire; but a sound account will send a man's soul to heaven. The Doctor asks the audience to say 'Amen' to all this; and then he departs, and the moral play ends.

NOTES AND GLOSSARY:

spouse: the soul as a bride entering into mystic union with Jesus was a common medieval idea

Hereabove: suggesting that the Angel may be speaking from a raised structure on the stage, possibly the same one from which God spoke at the beginning of the play

singular: either (1) personal, or (2) exceptional, or both

take it of worth: value it, take account of its worth

Save his Good Deeds . . . take: except for his Good Deeds, which he does take there with him

Ite . . . aeternum: see the Bible, Matthew 25:41: 'Depart, ye cursed, into everlasting fire'

Part 3

Commentary

IT IS GENERALLY ACCEPTED that Morality plays are a development of the medieval sermon. This may account for some of the ephithets which scholars have applied to *Everyman*: 'impressive lenten austerity'; 'grave'; 'solemn'; 'tragedy'. Yet the play is much nearer the classic idea of comedy than tragedy in that, despite alarms along the way, all ends well for Everyman. The fact that he dies does not, of itself, make the play a tragedy; far from it, the context in which death occurs in this play make Everyman's departure a triumph of hope for mankind. When Everyman accepts penance (the scourge) and shows contrition (the garment), he is half-way towards salvation; and when he takes communion, his redemption is assured. Thereafter, the possibility of tragedy is excluded. Humanum Genus in *The Castle of Perseverance* comes much closer to damnation: he dies unconfessed and in a state of sin, and it is after his death that his soul's cry for mercy and the intercession of the Four Daughters of God only just draws his soul out of the Devil's clutches. In the light of the Doctor's words at the end of *Everyman*, Humanum Genus is very fortunate:

> For after death amends may no man make,
> For then Mercy and Pity doth him forsake. (lines 912–13)

Tragedy has been avoided, but only narrowly. Christopher Marlowe (1564–93), a self-declared atheist, was later (1588) to portray with relish the figure of Doctor Faustus, who delays repentance so long that he is damned and he knows it. Here, the tragedy is fulfilled.

In *Everyman*, the opening speeches by the Messenger and God are intended to focus the audience's attention upon the universality of the action, and to emphasise the theme of transitoriness. The strong moralising of those speeches is balanced by that of the Doctor at the end of the play, who speaks with authority about the hope of redemption. All the action between is a simple journey.

In *Nature* and *Mundus et Infans* (?1508) the action covers most of the central character's life, and *The Castle of Perseverance* also follows the fate of his soul after death. In *Everyman* the action is confined to the close of Everyman's life, and this gives it a tighter dramatic structure than other Moralities. The point is made with telling brevity. We do not see virtues and vices competing over Everyman's soul: that past is conveyed to us through his relationship with Fellowship, Kindred, Cousin and Goods in much the same way as Hamlet's character before the opening of *Hamlet* is sketched by passing reference.

The main action of *Everyman* begins with line 85, when Death arrests Everyman in his tracks (possibly touching him with his dart), and continues unbroken until Everyman dies. He only gradually becomes aware of the reality of Death and of his own increasing isolation. His speech between his encounters with Goods and Good Deeds (463–85) comes in the middle of the play, and divides the action into two balanced parts. Everyman is here at his lowest and almost gives way to despair (a sin). Yet the speech is also a turning point, for he is about to enter into a dialogue with his most enduring friend, enduring despite his small past regard for her. The process of his regeneration has begun. Fear of damnation strikes Everyman (509–10) when Good Deeds proves too weak to rise from the ground and help him, and when she shows him his illegible or blank account-book. Yet he gradually gains in fortitude and, assisted by Knowledge, Confession and his Five Wits, moves towards a state of grace. He has still to experience the final desertion of his mental and physical attributes which God lent to him at his birth. This second set of desertions is an addition to the Faithful Friend story (see below) by the *Elckerlijc* author, or somebody before him, in order to make the point that a man ought not to depend on his own faculties any more than upon his worldly friends. It is his Good Deeds who eventually is strong enough to rise and go with him. In other Morality plays the prime importance of Mercy or Divine Grace is stressed. By placing the main emphasis in *Everyman* upon Good Deeds as the way to Salvation, the members of the audience are given a firm indication of the kind of direct human (and humane) action that they should take in this world in order to receive God's mercy in the next world.

Despite the intensity of the moral therein, *Everyman* was a popular play and has remained so. It manages to make its didactic point without resort to comic embellishments (unlike many an earlier Miracle play).

The source of the story

The plot of *Everyman* is derived from an old oriental (possibly Buddhist) parable, which was handed down to European Christians through the legend of *Barlaam and Josaphat*. The story is of a faithful friend who, when all others shrink away, stands by one who has received a strict summons to appear before a king. The tale was used by medieval preachers in their sermons as a moral example. One version of the story runs as follows:

And yet he said, that they that love the world been semblable to a man that had three friends, of which he loved the first as much as himself, and he loved the second less than himself, and loved the third a little or nought. And it happed so that this man was in great peril of his life and was summoned before the king. Then he ran to his first friend and demanded of him his help and told to him how he always loved him; to whom he said, I have other friends with whom I must be this day & I wot not who thou art; therefore I may not help thee; yet nevertheless I shall give to thee two cloaks with which thou mayest cover thee. And then he went away much sorrowful & went to that other friend and required also his aid; and he said to him, I may not attend to go with thee to this debate for I have great charge, but I shall yet fellowship thee unto the gate of the palace, and then I shall return again and do mine own needs. And then he being heavy and as despaired went to the third friend and said to him, I have no reason to speak to thee nor have I not loved thee as I ought, but I am in tribulation and without friends and pray thee that thou help me. And that other said with glad cheer, Certainly I confess to be thy dear friend and have not forgotten the little benefit that thou hast done to me, and I shall go right gladly with thee before the king for to see what shall be demanded of thee and I shall pray the king for thee.

The first friend is in possession of riches for which man putteth him in many perils and when the death cometh he hath no more of it but a cloth for to wind him for to be buried. The second friend is his sons, his wife and kin, which go with him to his grave and anon return for to attend their own needs. The third friend is faith, hope, and charity and other good works which we have done, that when we issue out of bodies they may well go before us and pray God for us and they may well deliver us from the devils our enemies.

This version was printed by William Caxton (?1422–91) in his translation (1483) of the thirteenth-century *Legenda Aurea* ('The Golden Legend').

The *Elckerlijc* dramatist (or an earlier writer) adapted the story so as to incorporate the medieval obsessions with death, the idea that human life is a pilgrimage towards the next world, the Dance of Death (grinning skeletons of the dead were supposed to partner the reluctant living in a macabre dance along towards the grave), and the Church's teaching on holy dying accompanied by the rites of the Church. The dramatist was greatly influenced by the long religious sermons and treatises of the time, particularly *Ars Moriendi* ('The Art of Dying') which was well known in Europe by the mid-fifteenth century. Caxton's abridged translations called *The Book of the Craft of Dying* (1490 and 1491) was probably known to the *Everyman* dramatist.

Thus it can be seen that the apparent simple directness of *Everyman* is a distillation of a complex background of ethnic, religious, moral and philosophical ideas.

The medieval sermon

To sit and listen to a long sermon is rarely easy, and medieval sermons could be very long—an hour, two hours, even longer. The sermon has always been the standard method of communicating ideas to a congregation, and Morality plays may be viewed as a development of the medieval sermon. Moral points could be made in a more interesting form: it was a way of 'sugaring the pill'.

Holy dying

Everyman is a dramatised sermon on the Catholic way of dying in Holiness and at peace with God. At the time of death, a man must give up any lingering desire for worldly possessions, accept that his physical attributes are all transitory, and put his trust in the good deeds that he has performed during his life. He will then be able to make a complete confession of his sins, do penance for them, and receive the last sacrament from the priest; and in this way he will die having returned to a state of grace in which his good deeds will ensure that his soul receives God's mercy and enjoys everlasting salvation.

Priesthood

Between lines 706 and 771 there is much Catholic teaching on the subject of the seven sacraments: baptism, confirmation, the ordaining of a priest, communion, marriage, extreme unction and penance. In this section Knowledge and Five Wits speak specifically in praise of priesthood. There is a passage in a medieval sermon which runs:

the which power [of a priest] neither archangel nor angel might never attain . . . . There is no earthly power equal to the power of priesthood. The power . . . of a king, or of a prince temporal, it goeth upon the body and upon worldly things, and nothing upon the soul. But the power that priests have . . . it attaineth to man's soul and maketh it both free and bound, quick and dead.

This bears a striking similarity to lines in *Everyman*:

There is no emperor, king, duke, ne baron
That of God hath commission
As hath the least priest in the world being. (713–15)

> God hath to them more power given
> Than to any angel that is in heaven. (735—6)

> The priest bindeth and unbindeth all bands
> Both in earth and in heaven. (740—1)

The same sentiments are present in *Elckerlijc*. Lines 740—1 mean that, by granting or withholding absolution, a priest has the power to decide the fate of a sinner in the next world.

However, Knowledge also points out between lines 750 and 763 that priests are not always as good as they should be: they are particularly guilty of simony (see note on page 37) and of breaking their vows of celibacy, thereby bringing illegitimate children into the world.

Knowledge's comments upon sinful priests are made after Everyman has left the stage in order to receive the sacrament and extreme unction from a priest; this suggests that his criticism and Five Wits' rather inadequate defence of priesthood in general are part of a contemporary concern about corrupt clergy. A debate over the role of the clergy had extended over the previous two centuries. In his *Canterbury Tales* (?1386—1400) Geoffrey Chaucer (?1340—1400) has little good to say of the members of the Church who are present on the pilgrimage to Canterbury, the Poor Parson alone being depicted as living according to Christ's teaching. In his tale the Parson attacks wicked priests and makes specific reference to simony, a sin of which the Poor Parson himself is certainly guiltless. Chaucer's Wife of Bath comments that no young girl out on her own is safe from the molesting hands of wandering Friars!

The last word on the subject in *Everyman* is that priesthood should not be condemned because some clergy abuse the office.

> Therefore let us priesthood honour,
> And follow their doctrine for our souls' succour.
> We be their sheep, and they shepherds be,
> By whom we all be kept in surety. (765—8)

The language

The language of *Everyman* presents no great difficulties. As with most good drama, the text 'plays' better than it reads.

The author (or translator) has struck a careful balance between a formal and a colloquial style of English. To find any kind of middle way was difficult at a time when the language was fast developing from medieval into modern English, and the present-day listener's/reader's ability to understand the diction with comparative ease is a testimony to the writer's achievement.

Repetition is sometimes used in order to emphasise a didactic point.

Between lines 111 and 143 Death repeatedly urges Everyman to lose no time in setting out upon his journey, and this gives the action urgency by working up Everyman's anxiety (and the audience's anxiety on his behalf). This is followed by reminders throughout the play that time is running out for Everyman (for example, lines 173, 192, 194, 569, 608, 866). Death makes a moral point concerning the futility of worldly wealth and the transitoriness of life:

> What, weenest thou thy life is given thee?
> And thy worldly goods also?
> EVERYMAN: I had wend so, verily.
> DEATH: Nay, nay, it was but lent thee.
> For, as soon as thou art go,
> Another a while shall have it, and then go therefro,
> Even as thou hast done. (161–7)

This is reinforced by Goods:

> What, weenest thou that I am thine?
> EVERYMAN: I had wend so.
> GOODS: Nay, Everyman, I say no.
> As for a while I was lent thee;
> A season thou hast had me in prosperity. (437–41)

Time and again during the play promises are uttered in language which reminds the audience of a previous promise. Fellowship says

> ...in faith, and thou go to hell,
> I will not forsake thee by the way. (232–3)

and then goes back upon his word, leaving Everyman to complain

> Why, ye said if I had need
> Ye would never me forsake, quick ne dead,
> Though it were to hell, truly! (254–6)

Kindred says (of Cousin and himself)

> In wealth and woe we will with you hold,
> For over his kin a man may be bold. (325–6)

but subsequently backs away upon hearing of Everyman's problem. This time Everyman laments:

> My kinsmen promised me faithfully
> For to abide with me steadfastly,
> And now fast away do they flee. (381–3)

Strength proclaims that he 'will by you stand in distress' (684), but later retracts, leaving Everyman to protest: 'Ye would ever bide by me, ye said' (815). The effect of this echoing is to underline the hollowness of all fair promises made by worldly attributes and to heighten a sense of dramatic irony—and also, in the examples cited above, of tragic inevitability (which is not to say that *Everyman* is a tragedy). Cousin actually warns Everyman:

> Trust not to me, for, so God me speed,
> I will deceive you in your most need. (357–8)

Many other words and phrases are repeated during the course of the play: e.g., *most need* (154, 358, 371, 523); *whole and sound* (625, 632, 916); *day of doom* (261, 885, 901); *heavenly sphere* (95, 695, 899).

These repetitions are there as a ritual emphasis, and are in no way an indication of limited vocabulary or lack of skill in using language.

During the first half of the play, Everyman relies heavily upon the wisdom of proverbs (a proverb is a brief saying which sums up a particular piece of common wisdom), for example: 'In prosperity men friends may find,/Which in adversity be full unkind' (309–10); 'Kind will creep where it may not go' (316); 'fair words maketh fools fain' (379). This reliance upon popular wisdom helps to make Everyman into an everyday sort of chap in the eyes of the audience. However, there are fewer proverbs in the second half of the play. This is probably a deliberate device to demonstrate that once Everyman's spiritual regeneration has begun he is less inclined to rely upon the kind of proverbial wisdom which has not always helped him in the past. In other words, he is now using his Five Wits and thinking for himself about the way to Salvation. At the same time, his style of speech becomes more high-flown and elegant as his spiritual condition improves. For example:

> O glorious fountain, that all uncleanness doth clarify,
> Wash fro me the spots of vice unclean,
> That on me no sin may be seen. (545–7)

The verse

Everyman was originally divided into stanzas. However, the verse is so irregular that no modern edition of the play attempts to reproduce those stanzas; instead, the text is printed in the form of continuous dramatic dialogue.

While some critics have condemned the poor quality of the verse, others see it moving towards the freely rhythmical lines of the golden age of Elizabethan drama which arrived some ninety years after the first performances of *Everyman*. The style of the verse in *Everyman* is closer to the rhythm of ordinary speech than is the more artificial verse of *Elckerlijc*. Strong emotion is expressed with simple, dignified power. T.S. Eliot (1888–1965) considered that the neutral verse style of *Everyman* allows the listener to attend not to the poetry, but to the meaning of the poetry'*. Eliot himself had the rhythms of *Everyman* in mind when writing his *Murder in the Cathedral* (1935):

> The rhythm of blank verse had become too remote from the movement of modern speech. Therefore what I kept in mind was the versification of *Everyman*, hoping that anything unusual in the sound of it would be, on the whole, advantageous.†

A.C. Cawley, the best-known modern editor of *Everyman*, sums up the versification of the play as follows:

> *Everyman*, unlike *Elckerlijc*, is very irregular in the matter of verse-length, verse-forms, and rhymes. The number of syllables in a line ranges from four to fourteen. The verse-forms are a welter of couplets and quatrains, together with occasional tail-rhymes, five-, six-, and seven-line stanzas, rhyme-royal stanzas, and octaves. (Varieties of quatrain 36–9, 86–9, 99–102, 103–6, 171–4; five-line stanzas 232–6, 262–6, 446–50, 526–30, 697–701; six-line stanza 206–11, 520–25; seven-line stanza 22–8; rhyme-royal 29–35, 131–7; octave 184–91, 880–7.) There are more than a hundred imperfect rhymes: some are examples of assonance and some are due to corruption of the original text, but this still leaves several pairs of words which fail to rhyme, as well as end-words without companion rhyme-words.... It should be said on behalf of the versification in *Everyman* that its verse-forms are not entirely haphazard. Some of the very short verses seem meant to mark a quick exchange of dialogue (for example 87–93), while rhyme-royal and octave are used in passages of exceptional gravity (for example 29–35, 880–7). These may be signs that the author-translator of *Everyman* is feeling his way towards a dramatic use of different verse-forms. Again, the rhyme-words are often skilfully distributed between two or more speakers, with the result that the dialogue is more rapid and flowing (for example 86–9, 97–8, 99–102, 675–8).‡

Characters

It might be more appropriate to entitle this section something like 'Human qualities'; for, as with all Morality plays, the characters in

* *Poetry and Drama*, 1950, reprinted in T.S. Eliot, *Selected Prose*, Penguin Books, Harmondsworth, 1953, p.71.
† *Poetry and Drama*, p.71.
‡ A.C. Cawley, introduction to *Everyman*, Manchester University Press, Manchester, 1961, pp.xxvii–xxviii.

Everyman represent types. Unlike many other Moralities, the worldly characters are not specific Vices, but represent acceptable human gifts such as good looks, friendship and prosperity which Everyman has abused by imagining that these gifts are everything. Fellowship, Kindred, Cousin and Goods can be regarded as his gifts of fortune; Knowledge, Confession, Beauty, Strength, Discretion and Five Wits as his gifts of nature. Arrogant in his security, he neglects his spirit: and in this circumstance, his worldly gifts prove unreliable.

There is no room for character development during the course of the play. Every type must behave within the limits of his name, for he is no more than a personification of that name. Unfortunately, this means that, while the conflict between good and evil provides a good story (therein is the basis for most good stories), dramatic interest in the characters is minimal. The playwright is using them to place before the audience a moral message, and he is not concerned with presenting them as real people. However, some are more vivid than others. All (apart from the Messenger, God, Death, the Angel and the Doctor) can be seen as aspects of Everyman himself; in this respect Everyman is the only 'character' in the play. The sex of each character is sometimes made clear in the text, but is usually left ambiguous—perhaps deliberately. All actors were, of course male (see Part 1 of these Notes).

The Elizabethan dramatist Ben Jonson (1573–1637) was later to create characters with specific temperaments or 'humours', but in his plays there exists an interplay of human relationships which is absent in *Everyman* and most other Morality plays.

Messenger

The Messenger acts as a prologue, previewing briefly the story and the moral to be drawn therefrom, and introducing God. He refers to characters who do not appear in the play (Jollity and Pleasure), and this has led some critics to consider that someone other than the main translator of *Everyman* added a prologue without careful reference to the text of the play. This may be so, as there is no Messenger nor any kind of prologue in *Elckerlijc*. Three other Moralities feature a Messenger with the same function as in *Everyman*, and several have a character called Prologue.

God

God appears as a character in only a few Moralities. He is traditionally represented as an ever-present figure whom Man tends to forget. As Death points out to Everyman:

Though thou have forget him here,

He thinketh on thee in the heavenly sphere,
As, ere we depart, thou shalt know. (94–6)

In *The Castle of Perseverance*, by keeping God out of the action until the very end, the danger is underlined of forgetting the One who sees all man's thoughts and actions and decides when his mortal life shall end.

Death

The role of Death in Morality plays is discussed on page 15, and the part he plays in *Everyman* is typical. However, in his 'Everyman, thou art mad' (168) he seems to become involved fleetingly in Everyman's plight. He soon returns to the role of a dispassionate observer.

Everyman

Everyman grows in spiritual stature as the play progresses. The playwright is encouraging the audience to admire the way in which he eventually faces up to Death. When he is first approached by Death, and told that his time is come, he is totally naive. He is astonished at the proverbial truths which never before had any reality for him: 'Death giveth no warning' (132); 'tide abideth no man' (143). He then almost falls into the sin of despair:

Alas, I may well weep with sighs deep!
Now have I no manner of company
To help me in my journey, and me to keep;
And also my writing is full unready.
How shall I do now for to excuse me?
I would to God I had never be get! (184–9)

However, he still has enough command of himself to realise that 'though I mourne it availeth nought' (193). He makes a brief appeal to God, and then begins to think positively in human terms:

What and I to Fellowship thereof spake,
And showed him of this sudden chance?
For in him is all mine affiance;
We have in the world so many a day
Be good friends in sport and play. (197–201)

As he is repeatedly disappointed in those he believed to be his friends, Everyman grows in philosophical strength and Christian patience. He manages to clear his mind of worldly matters and to move onto a spiritual plane before the actual moment of his entry into the grave. (For development of these ideas, see the specimen answer on page 59.)

Everyman is not meant to represent every human being in the world:

he stands for a typical Catholic Christian who is neither very good nor wholly bad. He loves the world too much, and regards his spiritual side too little; he is more human than the walking compound of the Seven Deadly Sins which is the nature of some of his equivalents in other Moralities. His fine clothes indicate how much he is in love with worldly vanity at the opening of the play; and his donning of the Garment of Contrition is a crucial step towards rejecting these things in favour of spiritual values.

Fellowship

Most Morality plays imply that all worldly relationships are at best vain and at worst criminal partnerships. Fellowship can be viewed as a potential—perhaps actual—criminal, and this seems to be supported by his willingness to commit murder (281–2) on the strength of his friendship with Everyman. Yet Everyman's reply ('O, that is simple [foolish] advice indeed!') implies that Fellowship's offer is not to be taken seriously, and that he merely wishes to demonstrate the force of his refusal to accompany Everyman upon his journey. 'A good fellow' was often a drinking companion, and by the sixteenth century this phrase had almost come to denote a rogue. We need not necessarily see Fellowship as such, but rather as a very human character who chooses to go on living at the cost of turning his back upon a friend. He will stay loyal 'In the way of good company' (214) and 'while the day is clear' (274); but his desertion in the face of adversity gives Everyman his first sure knowledge that 'In prosperity men friends may find,/Which in adversity be full unkind' (309–10).

Kindred and Cousin

After Fellowship has departed, Everyman makes an appeal to these semi-allegorical figures. Perhaps Cousin is not altogether unjustified in refusing to go with Everyman in order that he may attend to his own reckoning? Whether justified or not, Kindred behaves in the manner of human kind in this play: he lets down Everyman. He is shown as male in one early woodcut illustration of the character.

Goods

Goods reveals that he has all along been an enemy to Everyman, whose reckoning is the worse for his worldly possessions (see the Bible, Matthew 19:24, 'It is easier for a camel to go through the eye of a needle, than for a rich man to enter into the kingdom of God'). He laughs at Everyman's folly in thinking that all his goods are perpetually his (437—41). Goods is a thief and a traitor to a man's soul: love of possessions represents the deadly sin of Covetousness, which leads to damnation.

The likely staging of Goods is mentioned on page 54. It is notable that, like Good Deeds, Goods is immobilised by Everyman's attitude towards him:

> I lie here in corners, trussed and piled so high,
> And in chests I am locked so fast,
> Also sacked in bags—thou mayst see with thine eye
> I cannot stir—in packs low I lie. (394—7)

Everyman has bound his greatest friend to the ground and his worst enemy to his soul.

Good Deeds

Characterised as female, Good Deeds is Everyman's principal gift of grace. She is often measured by the degree of a man's generosity, which may take several forms. This is well explained in Chaucer's *Parson's Tale*:

> Now been there three manner of almes: contrition of heart, where a man offereth himself to God; another is to have pity of default of his neighbours; and the third is in giving of good council and comfort, ghostly and bodily, where men have need, and namely in sustenance of man's food.

Before Good Deeds appears, indirect reference is made to her (compare 'Alms' in line 78 with the words of Goods in line 432: 'to the poor give part of me'). In other Morality plays she is variously referred to as Alms or Charity; while giving of money is the most usual interpretation of both these words, they can also mean pity, tenderness, compassion. Charity is the main virtue in the play *Youth* (?1520) a point which the character Charity makes in his opening address:

> There may no man saved be
> Without the help of me . . .
> I am the gate, I tell thee,
> Of heaven, that joyful city.
> There may no man thither come
> But of charity he must have some.

Knowledge

Sister to Good Deeds (see lines 519—20) and hardly less important to Everyman, Knowledge, in her purest form, is knowledge of God

Nobody, said one medieval theologian, can go to Heaven 'without knowledge of God'. The highest form of human knowledge is self-knowledge, and it is self-knowledge in which Everyman grows during the course of the play, and which helps to prepare him to face his reckoning before God. He is led by Knowledge into acknowledging his own sin and towards the truth that 'they that I loved best do forsake me,/Except my Good Deeds that bideth truly' (868–9). As his awareness of his sinfulness comes to him, he is able to become humble as symbolised by his putting on the Garment of Contrition and his undergoing of penance.

Knowledge criticises sinful priests in reply to Five Wits' speech upon the honour due to priests.

Confession

Confession is probably the same character as the priest to whom Everyman goes in order to receive the last sacrament at line 749. The language through which this character is introduced (see lines 535–53), his single speech (554–72) and Everyman's reaction to the proferred scourge of penance (573–6) all stress the importance of Confession as a station on the way to God's grace.

There is some ambiguity as to the sex of Confession, especially if he is intended to be equated with the priest. When he first appears he is referred to as male by both Everyman and Knowledge (see lines 539–44). Yet immediately after this Everyman talks of Shrift—that is, Confession – as 'mother of salvation' (552). It has been suggested that Everyman is here using a figurative generalisation in the same way as he might refer to 'mother church'. However, the ambiguity is unsatisfactory. In *Elckerlijc* the equivalent character is feminine, and in *The Castle of Perseverance* Confessio is masculine.

Beauty

Beauty is the first of the gifts of nature to desert Everyman in the second half of the play. She is portrayed as female in an early woodcut.

Strength

Strength is specifically (and surprisingly) referred to as female in lines 827–8, yet is portrayed as male in an early woodcut illustration. This is not the first appearance of Strength as a dramatic character. Almost a hundred years before *Everyman*, Strength and Health appear as two knights attendant upon the King of Life in *The Pride of Life* (?1415). In that play, Strength promises to fight with Death.

Discretion

Portrayed in an early woodcut illustration as male.

Five Wits

Five Wits represents the physical senses of Sight, Hearing, Taste, Smell and Touch together with the inner sensibility of the mind. Knowledge calls to Everyman's mind that he will need to use his Five Wits in order to reach a greater understanding of his present position (662–3), and in this respect the senses must be applied to Knowledge if man is to interpret her (Knowledge) effectively. The importance of Five Wits is indicated by the fact that the playwright gives to him what amounts to a sermon on the key subjects of the seven sacraments (712–27) and priesthood (730–49, 764–70).

Angel

As agents of God, angels appear in many Miracle and Morality plays as heralds, ambassadors and suchlike.

Doctor

The Doctor acts as an epilogue, and the equivalent character in *Elckerlijc* is simply called 'Epilogue'. As a learned man who comes forward to expound the moral of the play, he is unique in English Morality plays. There is a similar figure in two Miracle plays, the Brome play of *Abraham and Isaac* and the Chester *Sacrifice of Isaac*. One 'Machabre the Doctoure' comes forward to underline the moral at the end of one version of *Dance of Death* (?1430) by John Lydgate (?1370–?1451), and a learned doctor appears in the same role in at least one German Morality play. All these commentators recall the preacher's firm voice pronouncing the medieval sermon which influences the whole shape of Morality plays.

The staging

There is some information about the general staging of Morality plays in Part 1 of these Notes (see pages 16–18), and *The Castle of Perseverance* is one of the few Morality plays about which we have much evidence concerning staging. However, a close look at the text of *Everyman* can tell us something of the style of its presentation.

There is no indication concerning any setting except for the central House of Salvation which dominates the action. The House of

Salvation in *Everyman* may be comparable to the castle in *The Castle of Perseverance*: in that play, the castle is the bastion of the soul of Humanum Genus, and the defences represent that state of 'vertus and grace' in which his soul stands after his repentance; in *Everyman* salvation, as represented by the House of Salvation, is the target of the action. Confession (that is, the priest) dwells in the House of Salvation, and it is possible that God spoke from the battlemented top of that structure. Audiences of Mystery plays were accustomed to seeing God set up on a high stage above the action (see page 10). From that perch the angel may also have sung at the end of the play his welcome to Everyman's soul. Perhaps Everyman's grave was located at the foot of the House of Salvation so that, after entering the grave, he could climb up through the House of Salvation to end up on top of it in the 'heavenly sphere' (899). As a place of confession, the House of Salvation may have resembled a church, with or without battlements. However, the general simplicity and intimacy of the *Everyman* setting may indicate nothing like as substantial a structure as that suggested above.

The properties to which there is reference in the text are Death's dart (76), Everyman's account-book (104, 502ff.), chests and bags belonging to Goods (395–7), the penitential scourge (561, 605) and the crucifix (778). It is probable that all these actually appeared as physical properties on the stage.

The only two references to costume in the text are the splendid clothes in which Everyman first appears (85–6, 614), symbolising worldly vanity and lack of care for inner values; and the 'Garment of Contrition', the penitential robe which he puts on after whipping himself with the Scourge of Penance. The change of clothes signifies a change of heart. This kind of costume change is a frequent symbol in Morality plays.

The entrances and exits of the characters in *Everyman* are such that a company of ten, or even fewer, can play the seventeen parts. Goods and Good Deeds, as a related pair of values, may have been present on opposite sides of the stage from the beginning of the performance.

Everyman has none of the dances, processions and music which enliven plays such as *Mankind*, *Wisdom* (?1475) and *The Castle of Perseverance*. Yet the simplicity—almost starkness—of the setting and stagecraft is exactly right for the basic theme and plain ritual of the play. Content, style of language and presentation are well harmonised. The play's single continuous scene allows no relief from the power of its message: the audience must sit (or more likely, at an open-air performance in the town square, stand) and watch the play from start to finish without a break.

Part 4

Hints for study

Preparing for the examination

In preparing for the examination you have probably read the play more than once; gone through it at least once in close detail, sometimes spending a whole session on the meaning, language, tone and other points of interest embodied in a single speech; and also, it is to be hoped, you have seen a performance of the play. The last is not always easy since performances of a set play, other than Shakespeare, are rarely available when you want them. If you are lucky, however, and hear of a production of *Everyman*, possibly one for which you have to travel a distance, it is worth making the effort to see it. Even if it turns out to be an interpretation of the play which you think is wrong—perhaps particularly if this is the case—it is valuable because you are driven back to reviewing the text and testing your view of the play against that of the director and cast of the production you have seen. Also, you have been reminded that what you are studying is a piece of drama and not a book; and that its verse is dramatic verse, intended to be heard rather than read.

As the day of the examination draws closer, you will want to find ways of bringing your knowledge and understanding of the text to a peak, without driving out all freshness of response so that there is no enjoyment left in it for you. If this happens there is a danger that your essays in the examination will be dull and mechanical.

Monotony can best be avoided by setting yourself varied tasks. Here are some suggestions:

(*a*) Spend some time reading through the entire play again, writing a series of symbols in the margin denoting different aspects of interest. For instance, you might write 'C' against words which illuminate facets of a character, either the speaker or another; 'I' could be written in the margin alongside a distinctive piece of imagery; 'T' adjacent to a notable theme which runs through the play; 'IR' for irony; and so on, inventing other symbols for any recurrent aspects of the play which you notice. When you have finished the play, make a list of references under different headings: this will help you to assemble your own thoughts and develop your own opinions.

(*b*) Commit to memory some useful *short* quotations—words, phrases, a few lines at most in each instance. You will find some useful ones used under various headings in Part 3 of these Notes.

(*c*) Write a paragraph summarising the plot. Then try to summarise it in two or three sentences. By comparing the two versions you can tell things about the dramatic structure. Which elements are vital? What have you left out in your second version and why? How much has the plot lost by your omissions?

(*d*) Ask somebody to start reading at random from the play: see how quickly you can identify the quotation, saying as much as you can about its context.

(*e*) Athletes train over the distance which they are going to run in competition: so should examinees. The examination will require you to answer a number of questions in a given time, and it is vital that you should accustom yourself to this pressure. Find out how long you will have to write each essay in the examination. Then sit down in a quiet place, choose a title for a test essay, and do whatever reading and note-taking you think necessary by way of preparation. When you are ready, put all books and notes away, get out pen and paper, set an alarm clock for ten minutes less than your allotted time, and commence writing your essay (see (5) below, under the heading 'In the examination'). When the alarm rings, you have five minutes to draw the essay to a conclusion, and five minutes to check it through for mistakes. Leave the essay and come back to it later. How does it read? Did you say what you meant to? Did you leave out anything? Did you include anything which now seems irrelevant and better left out? Ask a teacher or lecturer to assess your essay if you can.

After a couple of attempts at this exercise, you may feel strong enough to write two essays consecutively.

N.B. There is no point in the exercise unless you create examination room conditions for yourself. Write entirely uninterrupted: no background music and no getting up to make a cup of coffee in the middle.

In the examination

Here are some suggestions to help you in the examination room. They are numbered in order to give you a rough idea as to the sequence in which they may be considered:

(1) If there is a choice of question, consider carefully which will suit you best; but do not take too long to decide. Check how many questions you are required to answer on the paper as a whole.

(2) Read carefully your chosen question. If there are key words which you feel need clarifying, do that in the opening paragraph of your answer.

(3) If a question is in two parts, divide your time equally between the

two parts, unless you can show in your answer why one aspect matters more than another.

(4) Answer the question asked. However good your ideas, they are worthless if misapplied. An art examiner was once asked, if a candidate is asked to paint an oak tree and he paints instead a perfect cedar tree, what the painting is worth. The reply was 'Nothing'.

(5) Jot down a skeleton answer outlining the subject matter of each paragraph before you start to write the essay. As you write you may well find that new ideas emerge: be flexible and allow for these, departing from your plan if necessary. But if you start with no plan, then your essay will have no direction at any stage of its writing.

(6) Write legibly. An examiner probably has several hundred scripts to read: he will not be so well disposed towards a script which is very difficult to decipher.

(7) Keep your style clear and direct. Only use literary jargon when strictly appropriate; avoid impressive sounding but long-winded and empty phraseology.

(8) Unless the question specifies an account, avoid narrative; use it only when necessary to illustrate your argument. Merely to tell the story as an answer to most questions is virtually worthless.

(9) Do not quote long passages. It is rare to find that more than two or three lines are relevant to any particular point, and it is painfully obvious to an examiner when a candidate has learnt a passage and is determined to fit it into his answer, whether or not it is pertinent to the argument in hand. (N.B. 'Quotation' is the noun—not 'Quote', which is the verb.)

(10) There is no need to cite precise references. They are included in these Notes in order to help you to follow up and expand upon ideas. You will hardly be expected to have line references at your command.

(11) Refer to *Everyman* as 'the play' – never 'the book'.

(12) Never refer to a character as an 'actor'. While you should remember that you are dealing with a play, the term 'actor' refers to one who is playing the character, and not to the character him/herself.

(13) Only use a concluding paragraph if you have something more to say. You may wish to tie up some loose ends, or to assert a conclusion which you feel has not been sufficiently stressed; but it is a waste of time merely to repeat in summary what you have already said at length.

(14) Try to leave time to read through your answer, particularly if you know you are prone to make careless slips.

(15) The examination has a time limit. You should have worked out at the beginning how long you have for each question. Keep to your

schedule as closely as possible. It helps if you are ruthless over omitting unnecessary information, however tempted you may be to demonstrate to the examiner the range of your knowledge. If you do run short of time, resort to note form: display as much of your argument as possible, showing how the essay would have developed.

Questions

In the study of literature there is no such thing as a correct answer. Questions are asked in the spirit of debate and to see how well you can organise your ideas, and are not attempts to see if a candidate knows the 'right' answer. You should present all sides of an argument, and not merely the one which you favour. Give a structure to the way you display your knowledge and opinions, and *support what you say with close reference to the text*. Be disciplined: never allow yourself to get away with vague, general statements without referring to an appropriate part of the play in order to substantiate what you say. Quote where necessary—and remember that peppering your essay with single words or short phrases from the play in single quotation marks can be as effective as longer quotation. You should take the initiative and provide a focus when a question is very general: a question of this kind is usually more difficult than one on a specific aspect of the play, and it is easy to lose your way. N.B. The sections in Parts 1 and 3 of these Notes which are essentially background material (for example, 'The source of the story') are intended to help you to understand the atmosphere of the play. The information therein should be used very sparingly in an essay, and should never be allowed to crowd out a close consideration of the text.

The titles below are in no particular order, any more than the examiner will choose to ask you one particular question rather than another. Having thought about a title, you may wish to follow the procedure set out in note (e) of 'Preparing for the examination' above.

(1) 'The dramatic structure of *Everyman* is tight, and the didactic points are made with effective brevity.' Discuss how far this is true.

(2) What evidence is there in the play that Everyman has allowed worldly vanities to master him?

(3) Show how, as he is repeatedly disappointed in those whom he believed to be his friends, Everyman grows in strength and Christian patience.

(4) 'In *Everyman*, content, style and presentation are well harmonised.' Discuss.

(5) How far are the characters in *Everyman* dramatically interesting?

(6) What are the principal religious and moral points made in *Everyman*?

(7) Compare Everyman's preoccupations in the first half of the play with his preoccupations in the second half.

(8) 'The text of *Everyman* plays better than it reads.' Describe which aspects of the play you would emphasise on stage if you had the chance to direct a production of *Everyman*.

When you are confronted with the examination paper, the questions can seem different from anything you have seen before. However, it may only be the wording which is different. For instance, after you have read the specimen answer below, look at question (3) above: you will see that, despite the different wording, the question asked is very similar; but it is not exactly the same. Read again note (4) of 'In the examination' above, page 57. Ensure that what you write is strictly relevant to the question, and that you do not merely unload all the information you have about a character, nor just tell the story.

A specimen answer

Below is a specimen answer to question (7). If you would like to write an answer yourself on this question then you should do so before reading the attempt that follows. You will notice that elements from Part 3 of these Notes have been used, where appropriate; but they have been used sparingly, only the strictly relevant pieces being incorporated. Line references are given here as guides, but you would not be expected to remember them exactly (see 'In the examination', note (10), page 57 above). It is emphasised that the following answer is an 'attempt'. It is quite a good attempt, or it would not be worth printing here; but it must not be assumed that it is a 'model' or 'correct' answer.

---

(7) Compare Everyman's preoccupations in the first half of the play with his preoccupations in the second half.

When Death first approaches Everyman, he is aghast: the fine clothes which he is wearing at the time symbolise his attachment to worldly vanities. Also, his offer of a thousand pounds as a bribe to Death to 'defer this matter till another day' (123) shows how little he is able, at this stage in the play, to distinguish between completely different sets of values. Even Death shows a touch of human surprise at Everyman's sincere belief that his worldy goods permanently belong to him (168). Everyman's 'What desireth God of me?' (97) suggests that God is someone with whom he has had little to do during his life.

In Everyman's first soliloquy, after the exit of Death, he almost despairs, crying 'I would to God I had never be get!' (189). He briefly appeals to God for help ('Lord, help, that all wrought'—192), and later he calls upon the Virgin Mary ('Ah, Lady, help!—304) and Jesus ('Ah, Jesus, is all come hereto!'—378). However, all these appeals for divine help in the first half of the play are fleeting, and cannot be said to be genuine prayers. At this stage Everyman seems more prepared to rely upon the human folk wisdom enshrined in popular proverbs (see 309/10, 316, 413 and many other instances). He is still hoping to find his salvation in this world ('For help in this world whither shall I resort?'—306) and, after each short plea to Heaven, he turns towards worldly attributes—Fellowship, Cousin, Kindred and, finally, Goods. He is repeatedly disappointed (in Fellowship. 'Ye promised otherwise, pardie'—270; in Kindred and Cousin: 'I am deceived; that maketh me sad'—372; in Goods: 'Lo, now was I deceived ere I was ware'—435). When Everyman curses Goods and calls him a traitor (451–3) he cannot see that Goods has not deceived him—he has deceived himself through lack of understanding and self-knowledge.

He is also preoccupied with time: 'The time passeth' (192); 'The day passeth and is almost ago' (194); 'I lose my time here' (386). His past lack of care for his soul makes him terrified of the pain of hell which may be waiting for him: 'For now I fear pains huge and great' (190).

When all his gifts of fortune have let him down, Everyman utters a soliloquy which is both the crisis and the turning point of the play. At last it occurs to him that 'I shall never speed/Till that I go to my Good Deed' (480–1), and he begins earnestly to seek the aid of the one who will improve his standing in God's eyes:

> Good Deeds, I pray you help me in this need,
> Or else I am for ever damned indeed;
> Therefore help me to make reckoning
> Before the Redeemer of all thing,
> That King is, and was, and ever shall. (509–13)

The way Everyman talks of God here is more whole-hearted than in the first half of the play. He receives Knowledge in an assured—even relaxed—mood:

> In good condition I am now in everything,
> And am wholly content with this good thing,
> Thanked be God my creator! (524–6)

His language becomes more elegant and high-flown:

> O glorious fountain that all uncleannes doth clarify,
> Wash fro me the spots of vice unclean,
> That on me no sin may be seen.
> I come with Knowledge for my redemption,
> Redempt with heart and full contrition (545–9)

His fragmentary, despairing cries to Heaven have stopped, and he begins to address God with dignity and an understanding of moral and religious principles (581–604). In order to die in true holiness, he turns to mother Church to receive the sacrament and extreme unction (728–9).

As Everyman's salvation becomes sure he no longer worries about the passing of time—he is, after all, becoming secure for all eternity—and he is keen to go forward 'without tarrying' (651):

And now, friends, let us go without longer respite.
I thank God that ye have tarried so long.
Now set each of you on this rood your hand,
And shortly follow me. (776–9)

Also, he is no longer preoccupied with the pain of hell, but accepts with calmness the brief pain which he must endure before achieving eternal peace (528, 612–18, 628). His fear has melted away (654), but he still has to suffer the shock of the second set of desertions by Beauty, Strength, Discretion and Five Wits, his gifts of nature.

Stripped of all illusions and safe in the knowledge that his soul is redeemed, Everyman is able to turn to the audience and say:

Take example, all ye that this do hear or see,
How they that I loved best do forsake me,
Except my Good Deeds that bideth truly. (867–9)

Asking for mercy, Everyman commends his soul into God's hands and disappears into the grave with his true friend Good Deeds.

Context questions

A context question is one in which a passage from the play is reproduced in the examination paper, and you are asked one or more questions on that passage. If you are set one of these, remember that you must concentrate upon the passage set, and may only discuss matters concerning the play as a whole if the question invites you to do so. An example of a context test might be as follows: Everyman's soliloquy in lines 463 to 485 is printed in full. The questions which follow ask you:

(i) Explain briefly the exact context of the passage.
(ii) In what ways may this soliloquy be said to mark the turning point in the play? (see page 41 for some ideas.)

You may also be asked to explain briefly the meanings of certain words or phrases in the given passage.

Part 5

Suggestions for further reading

The text

There are many different editions of *Everyman* available in libraries. When these Notes went to press only two editions were in print:
The Everyman edition, ed. A.C. Cawley, in *Everyman and Medieval Miracle Plays*, Everyman's Library No. 381, Dent, London, 1956.
The New Mermaid edition, ed. G.A. Lester, in *Three Late Medieval Morality Plays*, Benn, London, 1981.
There are 921 lines in the play, and the line references in these Notes apply to all editions of the play.

Critical works on *Everyman*

There are sound critical introductions to most editions of the play. It does not matter if you cannot obtain any of the books listed below. It is *your* reactions to the play which matter. In any event, get to know the play well before embarking upon further reading; only then will critical works and background reading offer insights.

KOLVE, V.A.: '*Everyman* and the Parable of the Talents' in *Medieval English Drama*, ed. J. Taylor and A.H. Nelson, Nelson and University of Chicago Press, London and Chicago, 1972, pp.316–40.
RYAN, L.V.: 'Doctrine and Dramatic Structure in *Everyman*', *Speculum*, 32 (1957), pp.722–35.
VAN LAAN, T.F.: '*Everyman*: a Structural Analysis', *PMLA*, 78 (1963), pp.465–75.

Background reading

BEVINGTON, D.M.: *From 'Mankind' to Marlowe*, Harvard University Press, Cambridge, Mass. , 1962.
CHAMBERS, E.K.: *The Mediaeval Stage*, 2 vols, Clarendon Press, Oxford, 1903.
CRAIG, HARDIN: *English Religious Drama of the Middle Ages*, Clarendon Press, Oxford, 1955.

CRAIK, T.W.: *The Tudor Interlude*, Leicester University Press, Leicester, 1958.

CREIZENACH, W.: 'The Early Religious Drama', in *The Cambridge History of English Literature, Volume V*, Cambridge University Press, Cambridge, 1910, especially pages 51–60.

FARNHAM, W.: *The Medieval Heritage of Elizabethan Tragedy*, Blackwell, Oxford, 1956.

MACKENZIE, W.R.: *The English Moralities from the Point of View of Allegory*, Ginn, Boston and London, 1914.

OWST, G.R.: *Literature and Pulpit in Medieval England*, Cambridge University Press, Cambridge, 1933. See expecially the chapter on 'Sermon and Drama'.

POTTER, R.A.: *The English Morality Play*, Routledge & Kegan Paul, London, 1975.

ROSSITER, A.P.: *English Drama from Early Times to the Elizabethans,* Hutchinson, London, 1950.

SOUTHERN, R.: *The Staging of Plays before Shakespeare*, Faber, London, 1973.

THOMPSON, E.N.S.: 'The English Moral Plays' in *Transactions of the Connecticut Academy of Arts and Sciences*, xiv (1910), pp.291–414.

WICKHAM, G.: *Early English Stages 1300–1660, Volume 1: 1300–1575*, Routledge & Kegan Paul, London, 1959.

The author of these notes

NEIL KING was educated at Sherborne School, and at the universities of Durham and Cambridge. He has taught in schools in Stockton-on-Tees, Watford, Bushey and Cambridge, and has been an examiner in English Literature for five different examination boards. At present he is Senior English Master at Hymers College, Hull, and is engaged on research into aspects of moral and dramatic tension in Elizabethan and Jacobean revenge tragedy. He has compiled a drama series for schools which covers all aspects of the theatre from the Greeks to the twentieth century and has edited *She Stoops to Conquer* for Longman. He is the author of York Notes on *The Duchess of Malfi*, *The Revenger's Tragedy* and *The Changeling*, and has written and been co-author of plays which have been performed at Durham, Cambridge and the Edinburgh Festival.